Blessed Is the Man

A Man's Journey through the Psalms

Psalms of the Messiah

Praise the Lord!
Blessed is the man
who fears the Lord,
who greatly delights
in His commandments!
Psalm 112:1

Copyright © 2009 Concordia Publishing House

3558 S. Jefferson Ave., St. Louis, MO 63118-3968

1-800-325-3040 • www.cph.org

By Joel D. Biermann, Tim Radkey, Mark Burzlaff, Gary Dunker, Charles Strohacker, Joshua Salzberg, Lyle Buettner, and Matt Rovey

Edited by Robert C. Baker

Unless otherwise indicated, Scripture quotations are from The Holy Bible, English Standard Version®. Copyright © 2001
by Crossway Bibles, a publishing ministry of Good News Publishers, Wheaton, Illinois. Used by permission. All rights reserved.

Scripture quotations marked NASB are taken from the New American Standard Bible®. NIV®. Copyright © 1960, 1962, 1963, 1968,
1971, 1972, 1973, 1975, 1977, 1995 by The Lockman Foundation. Used by permission. (www.Lockman.org)

Quotations from *Reading the Psalms with Luther*, copyright © 2007 Concordia Publishing House. All rights reserved.

The definition of *Sacrament* on page 208 is adapted from *Luther's Small Catechism with Explanation*, copyright © 1986, 1991
Concordia Publishing House, pp. 202–203.

This publication may be available in braille, in large print, or on cassette tape for the visually impaired.
Please allow 8 to 12 weeks for delivery. Write to Lutheran Blind Mission, 7550 Watson Rd., St. Louis, MO 63119-4409;
call toll free 1-888-215-2455; or visit the Web site: www.blindmission.org.

1 2 3 4 5 6 7 8 9 10   18 17 16 15 14 13 12 11 10 09

Contents

Meet Our Authors

Joel D. Biermann

Joel resides in St. Louis, Missouri, with his bride of twenty-four years, Jeannalee. Their two daughters, Jasmine and Justine, are Lutheran school teachers, and their son Jess is enjoying his formative high school years. Joel's vocation finds him at Concordia Seminary, St. Louis, teaching Systematic Theology. Leading the list of favorite pastimes is any active outdoor pursuit with Jeannalee, who excels at providing what is best for Joel and their family.

Tim Radkey

Tim, his wife, Lea Ann, and their five-year-old daughter, Claire, reside in Lubbock, Texas, where Tim serves as senior pastor of Hope Lutheran Church. Tim has written and appeared in several DVD-based Bible studies produced by LHM's Men's Network. On weekends, Tim and his family enjoy spending time in the mountains of New Mexico. Tim also runs marathons, rides bicycles, and rides around town on his new Harley Davidson.

Mark Burzlaff

Mark is a first-time author who wants to be known simply as one who truly loves his Lord. A graduate of the University of Texas, Arlington, and Southern Methodist University, Mark is a staff manager with a national telecommunications provider. Mark lives with his wife, Amy, in North Central Texas and has one grown daughter, Allison. Mark is a member of St. Peter Lutheran Church in Roanoke, Texas.

Gary Dunker

Gary and his wife, Carol, live in Lincoln, Nebraska, where they worship at Messiah Lutheran Church. Gary works in sales for KLCV Radio, a member of the Christian Bott Radio Network. Gary enjoys attending Nebraska football and baseball games, writing adult Bible studies and dramas, as well as spending time with his four grandchildren Evan, Easton, Brynley, and Dathin.

Charles Strohacker

A native Chicagoan, Chuck is principal of Christ Lutheran School in Stevensville, Michigan. He and his wife, Diane, live in St. Joseph, and have two grown children: C.J. and Jennifer. Chuck's interests include photography, fishing, writing, and making people smile. And he is passionate about his Chicago Bears. Chuck maintains the Lutheran Education Association's blog at lutheraneducation.net.

Joshua Salzberg

Josh was a video manager for the 2007 Lutheran Church–Missouri Synod Youth Gathering and is a regular contributor to LCMS youth ministry publications. He works as a freelance film editor in Los Angeles, California. His wife, Sarah, is a theology teacher at Lutheran High School, Orange County.

Lyle Buettner

Lyle resides in Collinsville, Illinois, with his wife and three children. He is a member of Good Shepherd Lutheran Church in Collinsville and teaches Latin at Good Shepherd's school, where his children also attend. Lyle is employed at Concordia Seminary in St. Louis, Missouri. His hobbies include home improvement projects, home brewing, and spending time with his family.

Matt Rovey

Matt and wife, Alicia, and their kids, Karina, Carsten, Trevor, and Leah, live in Franklin, Tennessee, just south of Nashville. They are members of Our Savior Lutheran Church, where Matt also teaches Sunday School. Matt is a sound engineer, songwriter, and record producer and enjoys boating, camping, and traveling with his family. Visit Matt at myspace.com/mattrovey.

How to Use This Book

This isn't your father's devotional.

Then again, while your father may have not read the stories found in *Blessed Is the Man*, he may have heard stories similar to them. Stories told by his father or brother or friend, real stories from real men who experienced real life relying on God's real—and amazing—grace. Stories like the ones you've heard other believers tell you, or stories you've told yourself.

Blessed Is the Man provides you and your Bible study group with six weeks of faith narratives written by men who have prayerfully considered biblical psalms. At the beginning of each week, you will read an assigned psalm. Five days during that week, you'll read a verse or two of that psalm, followed by the author's story. Next, you may pray a suggested prayer or choose another as you see fit. Finally, you'll answer a few brief Bible study questions, which will help you consider other ways the psalm may apply to you.

To get the most out of *Blessed Is the Man*, prayerfully review the psalm from time to time throughout the week. Through God's Word, the Holy Spirit will confront and challenge, but He will also comfort and console. At the end of each week, join your brothers in Christ in a group Bible study. **Weekly small-group questions are reproducible.** So, if you want to hold your group Bible study before hammering the first nail at a Habitat for Humanity project, at halftime during a televised game, or before you throw the brats on the grill, do so! You may make as many copies of these pages as you need for the guys in your group.

We are grateful that you are taking a man's journey through the Psalms in *Blessed Is the Man*. Along the way, you may be reminded of stories of faith told by your grandfather, father, brother, or friend. The adventure into God's Word may even inspire you to tell a few of your own.

—The Editor

Suggestions for Small-Group Participants

1. Before you begin, spend some time in prayer, asking God to strengthen your faith through a study of His Word. The Scriptures were written so that we might believe in Jesus Christ and have life in His name (John 20:31).

2. Take some time before the meeting to look over the session, review the psalm, and answer the questions.

3. As a courtesy to others, arrive on time.

4. Be an active participant. The leader will guide the group's discussion, not give a lecture.

5. Avoid dominating the conversation by answering every question or by giving unnecessarily long answers. On the other hand, avoid the temptation to not share at all.

6. Treat anything shared in your group as confidential until you have asked for and received permission to share it outside of the group. Treat information about others outside of your group as confidential until you have asked for and received permission to share it with group members.

7. Some participants may be new to Bible study or new to the Christian faith. Help them feel welcomed and comfortable.

8. Affirm other participants when you can. If someone offers what you perceive to be a "wrong" answer, ask the Holy Spirit to guide him to seek the correct answer from God's Word.

9. Keep in mind that the questions are discussion starters. Don't be afraid to ask additional questions that relate to the topic. Don't get the group off track.

10. If you are comfortable doing so, volunteer now and then to pray at the beginning or end of the session.

Guide to Men's Ministry

There's a mother watching her boys play in the backyard. The boys are wrestling around in the mud, fighting to see who will be at the top of the pecking order, as brothers often do. There's another mother in the same backyard who has a little girl, or you might even say a *princess*. She comments, "Don't you think those boys are going to hurt one another? How are you going to get the stains out of their clothes?" To this the mother of the boys replies, "Boys will be boys." In this short story, it is clear that one mother understands boys and the other has no clue how boys become men.

The sad news is this: the Church in many ways has adopted the voice of the princess's mother who never raised boys. It seems men are expected to live, act, and behave in ways that make sure any remnant of their childhood has been extinguished. Men are tamed to fit the mold of what a good little boy should look like— free of danger, free of risk, and free of anything fun.

Giving men permission to be men once again is absolutely critical to the Church and to a successful men's ministry. There is enough boy left in every man that beckons to compete, have fun, risk, and live out the adventurous spirit only God can give. Yes, it is still possible for all of this to happen in the Church while men still live within the will and call of God in their lives.

7 Tips for Men's Ministry

GET "REAL" LEADERS

Men desperately need leaders who are authentic, genuine, and nonjudgmental. You must choose a leader that other men would want to hang out with and can relate to on multiple levels. This is a guy that other guys love to hang out with because he seems so down to earth, has fun living life, and would be a leader in any environment he found himself in.

THERA-PUKE-IC

Guys need to be in an environment that is natural, not clinical. Guys will share their struggles, challenges, and victories as long as it's not the purpose of the meeting or even the hidden agenda for their time together. When they catch wind that this is about to turn into group therapy, most guys will immediately button their lips, turn off their brain, and look for the nearest exit. When the environment is right, guys will talk. Don't force it. Please, don't force it.

LESS IS MORE

Women are always amazed at how simple men can be at times. Most men like simplicity and are drawn to it. Whether you're planning a men's social, Bible study, retreat, or small group, it is always better to err on the side of keeping it simple. Simple doesn't mean plain or boring; it means doing a few things really, really well. When you sit down to plan activities, try structuring them around broader themes such as having fun, learning a little, and providing a good challenge or risk for men to participate in.

TALKING IS OPTIONAL

Generally when men come together for activities, Bible studies, small groups, and/or retreats, there is going to be a time for prayer, reading, and answering some questions. There are many men who don't like to read out loud, pray out loud, or be put on the spot to answer questions out loud. Be sure to check with guys ahead of time about praying or reading. There will always be a few men who are comfortable answering questions, and these men usually pave the way for more timid guys to speak up.

KEEP THE SPIRIT OF COMPETITION ALIVE

Not all men played sports, but most men have competed as boys in some area or another. Men, by and large, enjoy competition and friendly wagers. Some men like playing golf against one another, while others enjoy seeing who smokes the best brisket. Either way you slice it, men always enjoy themselves when they can compete in a nonthreatening way, in a way that will never leave them feeling foolish in front of each other.

MEETINGS SHOULD NEVER BE MEETINGS

From time to time, there will be a need to plan various activities for men. The worst thing you can do is form a committee or a board. There will always be natural leaders who will need to do some planning for men's ministry, but have the meeting at a place men enjoy, like an athletic event, pub, or even on a golf course while playing a round. No one, especially men, needs to add more "official" meetings to his schedule. Make it informal and fun while you orchestrate real business.

A MINISTRY NEEDS MORE THAN ONE DOOR

How accessible is your ministry? The fastest growing churches always have multiple entry points for folks to get involved and be connected to their church. Men's ministry is no different. While there is a tremendous brotherhood among men, there are also a wide range of things that men like and don't like. Some men like camping and the great outdoors. Other men would prefer manual labor around the church. Some might even like more intellectually oriented activities. No matter what, you need to ensure that your men's ministry has many different attractions that respect different interests, gifts, abilities, and skills. There are venues for all men to come together, and there are activities that will only attract certain men. Keep all these nuances in mind.

3 Steps to Launch
a Men's Ministry in *Your* Church

LOCATION, LOCATION, LOCATION

Pick a place that will work for launching your first men's ministry event. A tailgate setting would be an absolutely prime site. Other options are at a lake, the rustic outdoors, or even a barn of sorts. Whatever you choose as your site, it should be a place where guys can get excited and loud and not feel closed in.

MEN EAT MEAT AND LOTS OF IT

Once you've got the location nailed down, it's time to think about the meat you are going to serve. Depending on what area of the country you live in, your choices and preferences will vary. Some examples are having a wild-game type spread of food. This usually takes place in areas where men enjoy hunting. If you have chosen a tailgate at some sporting event, cook up a bunch of bratwurst, brisket, and/or ribs. Warning: it's tough to cook a great steak when you're doing it in large numbers. Men are picky with their steaks, so be careful if this is your choice. Don't forget to bring beverages that your men would enjoy as well. (Okay, you can throw on some veggie burgers too.)

IT'S TIME TO LAUNCH—THE DAY IS HERE

Okay, you've chosen a great site. You've got the volunteers you need to cook the meat at the site. Now it's time to plan how you are going to effectively brainstorm what your men's ministry might look like. This is not a time to be critical of ideas. This is a time to really listen to what men are saying.

* What kinds of activities do they want to be involved with?

* What kinds of adventures are they looking for?

* What contribution do they want their men's ministry to make to the kingdom of God externally and their church internally?

Make this fun. For example, to get things started you could have some balloons attached to a big piece of plywood and have various ideas written on paper inside of the balloons. Have one of the men use the BB gun you provided to shoot one of the balloons and see what idea is inside and talk about it. This exercise can be a lot of fun, but please be safe with it. Once you have some good ideas about the direction the men would like to go, pick another location to flesh out more of the details and planning. Ask for any volunteers who want to help with this next phase. Once this next phase is finished, you should be able to get to work—but don't forget to keep on listening to the men in your church.

Introduction

"The Songbook of the Old Testament"—it's one of the standard appellations we give to the book of the Bible called Psalms. It is certainly not a bad title. After all, the 150 psalms in our Bible were written to be sung, and they are still sung every day, all around the world. Quietly chanted during family devotions, joyfully and boldly celebrated with organ accompaniment during the Divine Service, and even sung as a concert encore by U2, the Psalms appear and reappear with undiminished power and meaning. They continue to give voice to the yearning of the heart, the marveling of the mind, and the soaring confidence of faith. With poetry and poignancy, the Psalms are still helping God's people learn to sing the truth of God and His relationship with them. But "Songbook of the Old Testament" is, nevertheless, perhaps a misleading and restricting title.

Thinking of the Psalms as just a songbook contributes to a view that wrongly assumes the Psalms to be lightweight poetry lacking in doctrinal depth and short on meaningful application to real life. Granted, there are abundant examples of poetry that too quickly departs from the recognizable experiences of real life and soars into ethereal heights of irrelevance and . . . well . . . nonsensical confusion. Hard experience in high school and college literature courses has left more than one man wary of any composition labeled poetry. Enduring the reading of the poem is unpleasant enough, but the interpretation that inevitably follows hopelessly compounds the suffering of the poor reader, having as it does more than a little whiff of subjectivism about it—it is hard to escape the suspicion that it's all just being made up on the fly. So, (for good reason as it seems to me) poetry leaves many men cold. No surprise, then, that the Psalms, much less a study of the Psalms, the Old Testament songbook, might be met with indifference or even hostility by the average guy. To choose to read and study poetry stirs old and painful memories better left repressed in the subconscious.

That you have come even this far (the third paragraph of the introduction!) in reading and studying the Psalms is testimony, then, not only of your faith in God's Word to yield rich benefits to the reader but testimony also to your courage and capacity to hope: "Perhaps this time it will be better and the poems will make sense." That, of course, is precisely the goal of this study—or at least one of the goals. The pages that follow will tackle the Psalms head-on. Yes, *you* will be studying poetry! The Psalms *are* poetry. They *are* meant to be sung. Every psalm is a poem—a poem according to the standards of Hebrew poetry. Rhyming is only coincidental. More important in this poetry is rhythm, meter, assonance, imagery, and parallelism—most of which, sadly, is utterly ruined in translation. But even in English, without the full benefit of the beauty of the form, the Psalms still manage to convey God's truth—often in surprising ways.

This point deserves particular emphasis. While the form of every psalm is poetry, the content and message of different psalms varies considerably. There are psalms that delve into weighty questions of theology and that articulate fine points of doctrinal truth. There are psalms that give voice to the most acute sufferings of the soul. There are psalms that teach about practical life and provide guidance for mundane life. (Those "wisdom psalms" made up the collection covered in the first book of this series). There are psalms that rival the prophets in their ability to paint a vibrant image of the unfolding of God's future plan. The psalms that will be considered in this volume fall under this final heading. They are messianic psalms. They speak about David's greatest heir. They are prophetic, giving details—often startling details—about the character and nature of God's Messiah. They teach about the work and the glory of God's Chosen One.

Learning about God's Messiah, the Christ, is its own reward. Especially for the Christian, there is keen interest in knowing about God's plan of salvation as it was foretold and then as it began to unfold. A study of the messianic psalms needs no justification. Still, there might be an assumption (an erroneous one . . .) that while messianic psalms are good as far as they go, they aren't particularly practical or relevant. Some might, therefore, be reluctant to engage in a thorough study of these psalms, preferring instead to spend their time concentrating on parts of the Bible that are deemed more practical. If all goes as planned, however, as you spend the next several weeks exploring six messianic psalms, you will quickly discover that while they may be poetry, these psalms are neither irrelevant nor otherworldly flights of fantasy better at obscuring than illuming truth. The Psalms—even the messianic psalms—are rooted in the lives of real people (David, Moses, Asaph, and other anonymous writers) dealing with real problems and finding in God the surpassingly adequate answer to those problems. The genre is poetry, but the subject matter is sin, suffering, fear, failure, forgiveness, victory, celebration, confidence, and hope—the stuff of real life. The relevance for Christians today is immediate and multilayered. Indeed, if all goes as planned, your old ambivalence and suspicion toward poetry will be overthrown—at least when it is the poetry of these psalms.

Six messianic psalms have been selected, and then each has been divided into five portions. Each of these sections becomes the starting point and the guide for a brief devotional thought meant to shed light on the psalm and, more important, meant to make its application to real life vividly apparent. A series of questions will encourage you to further apply the message of the text to your own life experience. By design, the format is perfectly contrived to fit the pattern of daily devotions—one week's worth for each psalm. Finally, wrapping up the week's meditations, a series of questions is provided as a stimulus to learning and discussing in the context of a small group. Even without the benefit of a group's camaraderie and insight, however, the questions for discussion should help you to gain greater understanding of the psalm and its significance for your life.

The devotions are written by a collection of men like yourself—ordinary men with real jobs, real families, real struggles and real joys. These are men who face real problems: the fear and embarrassment of unemployment, the shock and turmoil of a daughter's unexpected pregnancy, and the heartache of pregnancy that ends in miscarriage. These are men who share the same joys as you: working with purpose in a meaningful and challenging job, the thrill and adventure of a cross-country road trip, the wonder of a star-filled sky, and the power of a summer storm. These men write about what they know, and you will recognize yourself and your own life realities in the experiences that they relate. These devotions bear no resemblance to the fanciful interpretations of poetry you remember from Lit class. They are accessible. They make sense. They ring true to life. They accentuate the relevance and practicality of the poetry we call the messianic psalms.

Besides the wealth of specific applications provided by the devotions, it is worth considering a few overarching points that will enhance your study of these prophetic psalms. First, the continuity of God's plan of salvation as it comes to fruition gradually and according to the divine timetable should be noted. Considering the grand sweep of the plan—it begins before God speaks the light into existence and extends until the glorious return of the Messiah—it is remarkable to observe the consistency with which God operates. As you read, notice the repeated appearance and reappearance of foundational theological themes (actually, doctrines!) such as the Creator's prerogative in choosing His people, the reality of human responsibility for every action, the believer's complete reliance upon God for all good things, and God's grace as the basis of every good and right relationship. These are the doctrines of Christian faith. That they norm and animate these Old Testament messianic psalms is testimony to the Father's singleness of purpose and reassuring reliability.

As you study each psalm, notice also how the portrait of the Messiah becomes more precise—and more wonderful. The Messiah keeps getting better. He is a king like David. He is a warrior ready to fight on Israel's behalf. He is a righteous judge who practices—and expects from others—absolute perfection. He is a lord whose reign will endure forever. He is the perfect priest who mediates between God and man. The description of the coming Christ expands until it becomes clear: no man can do this. Indeed, while the people of Israel kept waiting for David's greater Son, the reality kept getting worse. David had set the bar beyond the reach of any of his heirs. Josiah, Hezekiah, even Solomon—all fell short. No heir could rival David . . . until Jesus. And Jesus surpassed David. It would take more than a man to fulfill the messianic promise.

Finally, as you read, remember that through Baptism you are joined to Jesus Christ. Thus, what is said of the Messiah is said of you. What is promised to the Messiah is promised to you. What is done by the Messiah is done for you. Through faith, you are His brother. All He has He shares with you. The relevance of these messianic prophecies could not be more immediate or more personal. These are psalms about you and your future.

A transformative adventure awaits you. It's time to study some poetry.

Week One

Psalm 89:1–29

[1] I will sing of the steadfast love of the LORD, forever;
with my mouth I will make known Your faithfulness to all generations.

[2] For I said, "Steadfast love will be built up forever;
in the heavens You will establish Your faithfulness."

[3] You have said, "I have made a covenant with My chosen one;
I have sworn to David My servant:

[4] 'I will establish your offspring forever,
and build your throne for all generations.'" *Selah*

[5] Let the heavens praise Your wonders, O LORD,
Your faithfulness in the assembly of the holy ones!

[6] For who in the skies can be compared to the LORD?
Who among the heavenly beings is like the LORD,

[7] a God greatly to be feared in the council of the holy ones,
and awesome above all who are around Him?

[8] O LORD God of hosts,
who is mighty as You are, O LORD,
with Your faithfulness all around you?

[9] You rule the raging of the sea;
when its waves rise, You still them.

[10] You crushed Rahab like a carcass;
You scattered your enemies with Your mighty arm.

[11] The heavens are Yours; the earth also is Yours;
the world and all that is in it, You have founded them.

[12] The north and the south, You have created them;
Tabor and Hermon joyously praise Your name.

¹³ You have a mighty arm;
strong is Your hand, high Your right hand.

¹⁴ Righteousness and justice are the foundation of Your throne;
steadfast love and faithfulness go before You.

¹⁵ Blessed are the people who know the festal shout,
who walk, O Lord, in the light of Your face,

¹⁶ who exult in Your name all the day
and in Your righteousness are exalted.

¹⁷ For You are the glory of their strength;
by Your favor our horn is exalted.

¹⁸ For our shield belongs to the Lord,
our king to the Holy One of Israel.

¹⁹ Of old You spoke in a vision to Your godly one, and said:
"I have granted help to one who is mighty;
I have exalted one chosen from the people.

²⁰ I have found David, My servant;
with My holy oil I have anointed him,

²¹ so that My hand shall be established with him;
My arm also shall strengthen him.

²² The enemy shall not outwit him;
the wicked shall not humble him.

²³ I will crush his foes before him
and strike down those who hate him.

²⁴ My faithfulness and My steadfast love shall be with him,
and in My name shall his horn be exalted.

²⁵ I will set his hand on the sea
and his right hand on the rivers.

²⁶ He shall cry to Me, 'You are my Father,
my God, and the Rock of my salvation.'

²⁷ And I will make him the firstborn,
the highest of the kings of the earth.

²⁸ My steadfast love I will keep for him forever,
and My covenant will stand firm for him.

²⁹ I will establish his offspring forever
and his throne as the days of the heavens."

Mark Burzlaff

Psalm 89:1–4

I will sing of the steadfast love of the LORD, forever; with my mouth I will make known Your faithfulness to all generations. For I said, "Steadfast love will be built up forever; in the heavens You will establish Your faithfulness." You have said, "I have made a covenant with My chosen one; I have sworn to David My servant: 'I will establish your offspring forever, and build your throne for all generations.'" *Selah*

In All Circumstances

Over the course of my life, I've seen how people react differently to the way God intervenes in their lives. Some are happy and enthused by the experience; others are driven to tears. Some are open and receptive to changes in their lives; others become resentful. For some, the earth moves under their feet; others move out and take charge; while still others don't move at all. I've seen some people who are keenly aware of things and other people who are oblivious to what is going on. Some utter profound thoughts; others remain silent.

My own responses to God touching my life have covered the spectrum. I have been joyfully exuberant, like when my daughter was born. Even though we had been awake for twenty-eight demanding hours, I can still remember the exhilaration I felt upon seeing her for the first time. Her birth overwhelmed me, like someone carbonating my spirit and shaking it up before popping off the lid. I had never experienced such an emotional high before.

I have also grieved as I watched a church fail. Like observing cancer eat away at its victim, it was agonizing trying to lead a once-affluent congregation that was slowly losing its battle with declining membership, negative cash flow, and program cutbacks. Seeing a family of believers, like sharks during a feeding frenzy, turn on the pastor and then other church leaders was at best disheartening. As weeks dragged into months, God answered our prayers with a simple "No, I have something completely different in mind." This experience was a low I had never experienced before.

There have also been times when I have been utterly amazed. Although everyone goes through it at least once in their career, involuntary unemployment is nothing short of a kick in the pants. Having prayed about my job before it ended, God's hand in the outcome was evident, and I was optimistic. I did the normal things that people do: review my checkbook and savings account, look at opportunities to close gaps in our budget, and file for unemployment. In the grand scheme of things, God was in charge, and I knew that He had promised to provide for my needs. However, I still needed special help with some specific things, like a new computer that could print resumes and communicate with other computers. I also needed help with basic job-search strategies and tactics. Above all, I needed a new attitude.

I prayed earnestly, but in this situation and for the first time in my life, I asked specific yes or no questions of God. As respectfully as I knew how, I asked God to let me know what to do. I had heard about "laying out a fleece" but had never done it before. My grandfather had raised sheep, and I thought I still might be able to find one, but that would take weeks! So, as I lay pondering in my bed in the still darkness one early morning, I implored God to tell me what He wanted me to do. I thought about Gideon's prayer asking God to make the fleece wet but leave the ground dry. I wondered how God would accomplish that if He were going to do it. At that very instant, the briefest of rain showers, lasting no more than thirty seconds and doing little more than wetting the dry ground, burst forth. No thunder, no lightning, just rain, as if from out of nowhere. And just enough to "wet a fleece" but evaporate from the ground by the time I got there. After sitting straight up in bed, I woke my wife, telling her the story. That morning, I went to the computer store when it opened.

Paying for a new computer on a limited income was the next challenge. I didn't want to spend the savings I was holding in reserve for fear that my joblessness would outlast the severance I had received. Amazingly, the company that had terminated me called a couple days later and asked me to return temporarily to finish several items that hadn't been completed before I was let go. As it turned out, the wages from these extra efforts completely covered the purchase price of the new computer. Talk about answered prayer!

God also placed me in the midst of several Christians who not only helped me with job-search skills and resources but also helped me to see who I was and why God had created me the way He did. Further, they helped me focus on finding my vocation instead of just another job. As I met with them, we prayed that God would change my heart and put me in the place He wanted me to be. Needless to say, I found a job in a little more than six weeks. Most impressive, the job started on Monday, and the severance ran out on Tuesday. Surely we can sing of "the steadfast love of the Lord," and "make known [His] faithfulness to all generations" (v. 1).

God molded David and me, and He molds you using the circumstances and events of your life. David openly shared his hurt, frustration, and anxiety with the Lord. God encouraged David to come to Him with everything that bothered him in the same way a son goes to his loving father. David also expressed tremendous joy in receiving God's deliverance and salvation.

While we are separated from David by millennia, there is one thing we share with him: God's unfailing love in Jesus Christ. God kept His promise to David by sending His Son, David's descendent yet David's Lord. In Christ, God established "[David's] offspring forever" and built his throne "for all generations" (v. 4). Through faith in the Messiah, David recognized God's care and love in the midst of life's varied circumstances, both the good and the bad. That gave David great joy; David never ceased to praise our gracious King. Knowing God's "steadfast love" and "faithfulness" toward us in Christ, you and I can join with David in praising God too.

....

While we are separated from David by millennia, there is one thing we share with him: God's unfailing love in Jesus Christ.

Prayer: Lord Jesus Christ, when life seems to be going against me, or even when everything goes according to plan, be my constant guide. Help me to recognize that Your love and faithfulness are the strong cord holding my life and the lives of those I love together. In Your name I pray. Amen.

....

Monday

DAILY STUDY QUESTIONS
Psalm 89:1–4

1. When does God's loving-kindness seem sweetest: during good times or during challenging times?

2. Why is it that David focuses on his mouth as the fit tool for praising God?

3. Why is David so sure of God's loving-kindness and faithfulness?

4. Who is taking the initiative to establish the covenant between David and God?

5. How does a promise about David's "offspring" make a difference for us today?

Psalm 89:5–10

Let the heavens praise Your wonders, O LORD, Your faithfulness in the assembly of the holy ones! For who in the skies can be compared to the LORD? Who among the heavenly beings is like the LORD, a God greatly to be feared in the council of the holy ones, and awesome above all who are around Him? O LORD God of hosts, who is mighty as You are, O LORD, with Your faithfulness all around You? You rule the raging of the sea; when its waves rise, You still them. You crushed Rahab like a carcass; You scattered Your enemies with Your mighty arm.

Wonder of Wonders

I can only imagine the composition of the heavenly praises mentioned in verses 5–10. I visualize Hollywood-style special effects replete with jolting flashes of lightning accompanied by peals of thunder; voices reverberating tones of a thousand clashing cymbals; trumpets and angel choirs; and the breathtaking awe of the glory of Almighty God. But the grandeur of heaven's praise, as great as it must be, must pale in comparison to the regal splendor of God's love and faithfulness in the lives of His people (see 1 Peter 1:10–13). While facing what equates to their darkest hours on this earth, God's very own testify to His magnificent calming of the storms in their lives and witness His incomparable might as He defeats their greatest enemies.

Bob, a long-time friend of the family, was one of my mentors. Already retired, he fit between my grandfather and father in age and had a worldview that pointed everyone he met to Jesus. As a young man, he had been on the Navy boxing team, a fact testified to by his grip of steel. His nose was somewhat misshapen, he said, after being broken in his last match by a right hook he never saw coming. Despite his outward appearance, he was warm and outgoing, compassionate and thoughtful, yet strong and resolute even in difficult times. He always had a smile and the time to talk. He was one of the most influential men I have ever known. Most never knew how he struggled over a physically challenged son who was confined to a nursing home half a continent away and with whom he deeply regretted not being able to share moments as the father he wanted to be.

Ellen was our next-door neighbor. She was older and widowed, but had remarried. Ellen was part of my and my wife's support network, always willing to lend a hand, offer helpful advice, or just be a friend when one was needed. Unfortunately, Ellen faced a dark night of her own when her marriage ended in divorce. She struggled but with the Lord's help was healing. Toward what should have been the end of the healing process, Ellen's daughter committed suicide. She had been Ellen's pride and joy, a pretty girl, popular and outgoing, very much a vivacious twenty-year-old. What wasn't apparent was the war that had raged in her daughter's mind as a result of Ellen's divorce. After agonizing for the three days that her daughter was missing, the news of her daughter's death was finally confirmed, and Ellen was devastated. Excruciating wounds that had started to heal were ripped open again, and bitter exchanges with her ex-husband seemed too much to bear.

But Ellen was a woman of faith. The Lord held her, cared for her, and helped her through the pain to a place of healing and grace. As I think back on the events of those trying months, I am still heartbroken by the pain we witnessed and sometimes shared with her. I offer praise, however, to Ellen because of her witness to God's grace. She didn't pull herself up by her own bootstraps and would never tell you she was a self-made woman. She was simply a broken individual who by faith clung in her agony to the only thing she had to cling to: her Lord.

Steve was a member of our congregation, and I was honored to talk with him about his spiritual walk. Steve was a typical Christian young man who was intelligent, well spoken, and of good character. As recent college graduates, however, he and his wife had followed her career path, which at the time had presented a better opportunity. Coming from a conservative, traditional background, it was difficult for Steve to face not only the disappointment of having his career put on hold but also the criticism and seeming ridicule of being a stay-at-home husband. Several odd jobs hadn't worked out, and he was struggling to find God's plan for his life.

After my family moved, I lost touch with Steve until I ran into him recently. He had become a pastor and now was a vibrant image of Christ's love, a beacon for the Gospel. He was sure of himself and the message he boldly proclaimed. I was amazed to see how God had moved this man to being a powerful full-time witness for Him. In the course of our conversation, I shared some of the difficulties I was having with my current job. Due to cutbacks and downsizing, I was feeling guilty over having to fire employees who had devoted their lives to building the company. Instead of trying to analyze my problem or suggest remedies to fix it (my way of helping a friend), he reassured me like someone who had walked in similar shoes. He simply said, "You are forgiven." As he repeated the message, he continued, "Sometimes the first words you need to hear are that Jesus loves you and died for you and that you are forgiven. Sometimes those are the only words you need to hear." I remember being overwhelmed by the simplicity and power of the three simple words. And he was right.

God obviously worked in the lives of these individuals as He shepherded them through their difficult times, and at the same time He used them to profoundly influence me. While my life was dramatically affected by these three individuals, I know none of them would consider their actions as being profound. They simply walked by faith through the hills and valleys God placed in front of them. As we consider God's work in our lives, it is good for us to consider the image that God is endeavoring to create in us, the image of His Son.

Sometimes we are blinded by the mountaintop experiences of God's power and might. But we really don't need a Hollywood-style production to prove God's faithfulness and love. Rather, we are called simply to trust in our wonderful, faithful, incomparable Lord, who crushed sin, Satan, and death for us on the cross. Confessing with our lips and our lives that our fearful, awesome, and mighty God provides exactly what His children need is the greatest praise we can offer.

....

Sometimes we are blinded by the mountaintop experiences of God's power and might. But we really don't need a Hollywood-style production to prove God's faithfulness and love.

Prayer: Heavenly Father, I praise You for Your power and glory. Chiefly I praise You for Your boundless grace and mercy to me, a poor sinner, through Your Son, Jesus Christ, my Lord. Amen.

....

Tuesday

DAILY STUDY QUESTIONS
Psalm 89:5-10

1. Who are some ordinary Christians who have, without even knowing it, made an extraordinary impact on your life?

2. Is it possible that you have made an extraordinary impact on another Christian without even knowing it? Is this a goal that you can choose to pursue?

3. Verses 5–8 picture a gathering of "holy ones" that surpasses the sort of mutual associations we know. How would this heavenly gathering differ from our gatherings at church? How might it be similar?

4. What evidence does David offer for Yahweh's ("the LORD's") unsurpassable and incomparable being?

5. David seems to delight in the crushing of Egypt and the scattering of God's enemies. Is such an attitude appropriate for Christians today?

Psalm 89:11–18

The heavens are Yours; the earth also is Yours; the world and all that is in it, You have founded them. The north and the south, You have created them; Tabor and Hermon joyously praise Your name. You have a mighty arm; strong is Your hand, high Your right hand. Righteousness and justice are the foundation of Your throne; steadfast love and faithfulness go before You. Blessed are the people who know the festal shout, who walk, O Lord, in the light of Your face, who exult in Your name all the day and in Your righteousness are exalted. For You are the glory of their strength; by Your favor our horn is exalted. For our shield belongs to the Lord, our king to the Holy One of Israel.

A Mighty Arm, a Strong Right Hand

Creation acknowledges God as the owner and founder of everything that is. It is hard not to be in awe of His marvelous works when contemplating His creation. Whether looking across the West Texas desert nearly one hundred miles into Mexico from the South Rim of Big Bend National Park or peering into the vast expanse of the Grand Canyon from the North Rim, whether in the Rockies or the Sierras, God's splendor is easy to see. In God's greatest creation, however, one sees a demonstration of not only His splendor and might but also His mercy and fatherly love for a people crafted in His very image.

God's people are truly the highlight of His creation. God has lifted high the right arm of His only Son, our Lord, and in so doing, He has set His rule of righteousness and justice attended by love and faithfulness. As a result, we are truly blessed. We walk in the light of His face. We are filled with joy and pride because of His righteousness. We find strength in His glory. We take refuge in Him, and we rejoice with all of creation in His name. It is a truth of reconciliation: a people created by the one true God, lost as the result of their sinfulness, facing eternal death and damnation, are now redeemed by the sacrifice of Jesus Christ, whose sufferings, death, and resurrection resulted in forgiveness and regaining life with Him. It is also a truth about a heavenly Father who cares for His children, watches over them, protects them, and molds them into the likeness of His Son.

On a trip from our Texas home to my in-laws' house in Iowa, my wife and I were looking forward to a couple of days off. Riding with us was my daughter, who was looking forward to spending time with Grandpa and Grandma. It was the Thanksgiving weekend. Normally, the trip took twelve hours by car. We usually traveled without stopping, lacking resources for a hotel room or airplane ticket. That Thanksgiving, we were also short on time, and the weather wasn't cooperating. A cold front was moving across the Midwest, bringing freezing temperatures and threatening to making conditions hazardous. Light rain began mixing with sleet and freezing as it fell. With the encroaching darkness, temperatures dipped below freezing, only to get worse as the evening progressed.

We were in the final stretch of interstate highway, someplace between Kansas City and the Iowa border, when road conditions deteriorated further. I thank God still today for His provision that night. We had been pushing to get to our destination, praying that the roads and weather would hold out for the duration of our trip. If they did, we would arrive late in the evening. If not, we might not get there at all.

Suddenly, I noticed a change in the sound of the tires on the pavement. I'm not sure exactly how, but I quickly realized that something was different. Instinctively, I slowed down. Mentioning to my wife what I believed had just happened, we adjusted our seat belts. As we crossed over the next hill, emergency lights were flashing and cars that had passed me at full speed only moments before were lying in a ditch.

Sometime later, we noticed that it had begun raining again and surmised that we had gotten in front of the freezing weather. After I relaxed a little, I called out to my daughter in the backseat, "Are you still there? I wanted to make sure we hadn't lost you someplace; you've been so quiet."

"Yes, Daddy," she chimed back. "You know that I am. I'm right here with you."

I was very much amazed that night—first, by God's provision and protection. After a full day of driving, I'm not normally attuned to a slight change in the pitch of tires on a roadway. I was amazed that I even noticed the change, moreover was moved to take instant action, which I believe averted what could have been a disaster. Second, I was awed by my daughter's response of faith. Glancing back at her in the rearview mirror, I could tell that she was aware of the danger and that the flashing lights had concerned her. I certainly was more than just a little nervous about driving on icy roads. She, in contrast, had relaxed into her father's and her heavenly Father's care, and she did it much sooner than I had.

I'm glad to be numbered among the saints as a believer in Jesus Christ. As my Redeemer, God has extended me that opportunity and called me to be one of His own. I am part of His vast creation (v. 11), and He has rescued me with His mighty arm and strong right hand (v. 13). His steadfast love and faithfulness were proved to me on Calvary. Now He makes sure that I'm safe and taken care of in troubled times. When I call upon Him, He answers. He is the Good Shepherd who leaves the other ninety-nine sheep in open pasture so He can find me.

How can we respond to such grace? By living our lives according to the same precepts of righteousness and justice attended by love and faithfulness. No matter what our position, as we consider the struggles of our lives, whether at the job, in the marketplace, or as a husband and parent, maybe it would be better to stop asking if we're "there" yet when the answer hasn't changed. Instead, He wants us to take refuge in Him and rest assured in His promises. As one of His own, He desires that we look to Him in times of trouble in much that same way my daughter responded to me that night: "Yes, Father, I'm right where I should be, here with You." Next to Him, we, too, rejoice with all of creation that we belong to "the LORD, our king . . . the Holy One of Israel" (v. 18).

> How can we respond to such grace? By living our lives according to the same precepts of righteousness and justice attended by love and faithfulness.

> *Prayer: Dear Lord, thank You for Your gracious providence and for protecting me from all harm and danger. Mercifully forgive me for relying on my own strength, and grant me a right spirit that praises Your holy name. For Jesus' sake. Amen.*

Wednesday

DAILY STUDY QUESTIONS
Psalm 89:11–18

1. When was a time when you barely missed some potential disaster? Did you experience an unusual intervention of awareness or warning?

2. David was understandably impressed with some of the mountains of Israel (v. 12). What are some of the wonders of nature that help remind you of God's character and His care for you?

3. Why are righteousness and justice excellent materials for the foundation of a throne?

4. What does it mean to walk in the light of God's face or under His kind gaze?

5. Is it right for "Holy One of Israel" to be capitalized? Can you also claim Him as your king?

Psalm 89:19–23

Of old You spoke in a vision to Your godly one, and said:
"I have granted help to one who is mighty; I have exalted one
chosen from the people. I have found David, My servant; with
My holy oil I have anointed him, so that My hand shall be
established with him; My arm also shall strengthen him. The
enemy shall not outwit him; the wicked shall not humble him. I
will crush his foes before him and strike down those who hate
him."

Chosen and Anointed

When I think about David being chosen and anointed, I see him adorned in the finest array, returning victorious from battle with a laurel wreath on his brow. But Scripture tells us a different story. David was a sinner in need of grace, just like I am, just like you are. David experienced God's faithfulness, mercy, and forgiveness. David's splendor did not earn God's favor; rather, God blessed David with the provision of His hand. God did the choosing, anointing, and supporting. However, God did this not only for the greatest king on earth but also for you and me. By the power of the Holy Spirit, God chose us and anointed us with His grace through the Gospel. He continues to support us brothers of His Son, the greatest king in all of eternity. Through Jesus, He gives us the victory and as a result, the opportunity to live with Him forever.

I don't remember when God chose me (actually it happened in eternity, before the world began; see 2 Thessalonians 2:13 in the NIV), although I know I was chosen and called by the Holy Spirit to faith in Jesus Christ. His Spirit dwelling in my heart is God's guarantee. I don't remember my anointing either, although there are people who witnessed my Baptism, when God staked His claim of ownership over me. It's not that I don't want to remember; I simply can't.

Growing up in the Bible belt of the South, I frequently heard about the necessity of having a "conversion experience." This experience signified that one had been saved from a life of sin and was now journeying into eternal life because of one's decision to follow Jesus—though that somehow was also a gift of God's grace. Some believed that if you didn't have of these experiences, you probably weren't saved. I frequently felt out of place among my friends who believed this because I couldn't remember my Baptism and had never had a conversion experience. Not that my friends ever put me down or were ever skeptical of my faith in Jesus Christ, there was just an uncomfortable difference that was awkward to explain. My friends couldn't understand why I didn't have a dramatic testimony of conversion in my life. Explaining my beliefs at thirteen was difficult, and to people who had no idea what you were talking about, it was next to impossible. There was simply a fundamental difference in how we talked about faith.

My friends talked about their lives in the church, going to Sunday School, and studying God's Word, just like me. They talked about praying at home before meals and at bedtime, just like me. They even talked about youth groups and summer retreats, just like me. But when it came to their conversion, they talked about coming to a recognition of their need for a Savior, followed by a public repentance and a statement of faith. Then they were baptized. Some talked of even being immersed in a river, just like Jesus.

When did I first come to know that I was a sinner in need of Jesus? When did I pray that Jesus would come into my heart and be my Lord and Savior? When did I know that I was a Christian?

I had been baptized as a young baby and didn't remember anything about the event of my Baptism. While I knew I was a sinner and needed Jesus, there was never a time that I suddenly became aware of it. I couldn't remember a time when I didn't know the Lord. I had no testimony of a conversion experience. I felt like a fifth wheel in most faith discussions.

Later in life, I discovered that my family heritage included more than six generations of Lutheran Christians. A major component of our family heritage, it turned out, was a legacy of faith passed down from one generation to the next. I'm not suggesting that anyone receives salvation based on the actions of their ancestors or even their own. Saving faith in Christ Jesus is a free gift extended to us through God's grace by the Holy Spirit. For me, the blessing was a chain of grace received through Word and Sacraments that continued across multiple generations without interruption. This unbroken chain of grace, another friend explained, was a blessing that I should make certain was passed on to my children. It is not a guarantee, he said, but rather a gift that we should take seriously, value highly, and treat with the greatest of respect.

Now I see that my blessing is something to be proud of. Lacking a conversion experience no longer concerned me. Even now, as my daughter faces some of the same questions I had when I was young, I tell her not to be concerned because she cannot remember her Baptism. Instead, I share with her that her mom and dad can't remember theirs either. Neither could her grandparents, her great-grandparents, her great-great-grandparents, all the way back to her great-great-great-great-great-grand-parents. But all of these people believed with all their hearts that Jesus died and rose from the dead for them. They earnestly loved Him and prayed diligently for their family, including her. They were diligent also to take hold of the gifts of the Holy Spirit, stress the importance of faith in Jesus Christ to family members, and secure the active participation of future generations by passing on the faith that has become a legacy for all of us. I shared with her, too, the future joy of being able to meet all of them in heaven, including those neither of us has ever seen.

The victory that was promised to David, the victory that was fulfilled in Christ, is extended to you and me in the words of this psalm. This victory is real. I am confident that my childhood friends, like my forefathers and mothers, will be with me in heaven on the Last Day. I sometimes think about them and the testimony I didn't have the opportunity to share with them as a youth. I'm proud of the legacy God has blessed me with, however, and I thank Him for doing it the way He did. I wouldn't want it any other way. The victory He promised us is ours through Jesus. And it's a victory worth celebrating.

....

The victory that was promised to David, the victory that was fulfilled in Christ, is extended to you and me in the words of this psalm.

Prayer: Heavenly Father, thank You for choosing me before time began, for calling me to faith through the Gospel, and for anointing me with Your Spirit in my Baptism. By Your grace, help me to live a life worthy of my heavenly calling. I ask this in Jesus' name. Amen.

....

Thursday

DAILY STUDY QUESTIONS
Psalm 89:19-23

1. What's the most exhilarating sensation of pure victory that you have experienced?

2. In your own life right now, are you feeling the flush of victory, or the continued agony of the struggle?

3. What kind of connection do you, a twenty-first century Christian, have with David an ancient king of Israel?

4. Are there any forces of wickedness or enemies at work in your life making things miserable for you?

5. How are we to react to those who seem intent on stealing from us the joy of life?

Psalm 89:24-29

My faithfulness and My steadfast love shall be with him,
and in My name shall his horn be exalted. I will set his hand
on the sea and his right hand on the rivers. He shall cry to Me,
"You are my Father, my God, and the Rock of my salvation."
And I will make him the firstborn, the highest of the kings of
the earth. My steadfast love I will keep for him forever, and My
covenant will stand firm for him. I will establish his offspring
forever and his throne as the days of the heavens.

Our Father, Our Rock

Verse 26 takes us to the climax of the psalm, a promontory that reveals the fulfillment of God's promises to David in our Savior, Jesus Christ. Through faith in Him, it also reveals God as *our* Father and *our* Rock. This is a common theme throughout Scripture: God is the Rock of Israel, the Rock of salvation, and the Rock upon which He builds His Church. The imagery of God as the mighty fortress, a stronghold against all that would assail us, is vivid, as is the image of God as a precipice that stands tall and bold, incomparably higher and greater than all the rest.

God is the Rock that marks my path and guides my way through the dreary, fog-laden avenues of this life. He is the Rock that I lean on when dark times engulf me, the island in the midst of rushing waters, and the bridge that spans the divide between us. His love is without measure, and also without end. His love is sometimes beyond belief, yet it comforts and soothes as it draws me to Him. His gift of faith is alive within me, something that I alone am incapable of. This faith also generates a response, a desire to give my all to Him and for Him and to be used by Him for the purpose He sees fit. It's a desire to trust Him in everything in this life and to tell of His love and faithfulness as it bears out on the life story He has given me, even if I don't understand exactly why.

In high school, I hung out with a group of friends who typically met during lunch and off periods. One member of our group was a nonbeliever who was enamored with a girl from a very fundamentalist Christian family. One day, he asked,

"What's this Christianity stuff all about, anyway?"

His question, posed so directly, took me aback. But leaning forward in my chair, I answered him. Christianity is about Jesus and why we needed a Savior. I told him that we were sinners, incapable of earning or holding God's favor. In fact, we were destined for eternal separation from God because of our failing to live up to God's standards. I told him that God wanted us to experience a different outcome, but because of His holiness, the sin had to be dealt with. Jesus was God's solution to the problem; it was His sufferings and death on the cross that paid the price for our sinfulness. And it was His resurrection from the dead three days later that reconciled us to God and made it possible for us to live with Him in heaven for all of eternity. I told him that this eternal life was not something that could be bought or earned. It was a free gift from God that could be his if he believed. I had to say, it was the most perfect presentation of the Gospel I could muster. But at the end of the conversation, he thanked me and walked way.

"So much for that opportunity," I thought. However, another friend who unbeknownst to me had listened to this conversation came to me several days later.

"Wow!" he said. "It was so amazing to hear what you said. I had heard that all of my life, and I knew the Bible. But it had never been so clear or organized before. It never made so much sense."

Another time, I shared the Gospel with a family friend, who unfortunately hadn't asked and got more than he bargained for. I pelted him with fire and brimstone and hammered him about his need for the Gospel. I felt him recoil and experienced an abrupt end to the conversation. The Lord showed me that day how my plan wasn't necessarily His plan. I thought long and hard about how Jesus would have handled that encounter. Maybe He would have treated this young gentleman with the same style as He did the woman at the well or like He did Zacchaeus or maybe like He did the Roman centurion. Absolutely, He wouldn't have treated him the way that I did. Fortunately, I had the opportunity to talk to this friend again, but this time in a way that was more like Jesus. We talked about what was going on in his life. I listened to his struggles and heard about his successes and disappointments. We talked at length about his dreams and aspirations and how there seemed to be so many directions for him to follow. He confided that he was nervous about picking the one that was best. I shared with him how I had similar struggles as a young man and how the Lord had given me a purpose and a direction. I'll never forget the sense of longing and concern I had for this friend as I shared with him the second time and how I felt the Lord's love and compassion for him. Equally impressive to me, my witness was not one of convincing rhetoric but of two ears tuned to the needs of a crying soul.

Over time, God has taught me that my behaviors and attitudes articulate what I believe to those who are watching and listening much more clearly than what I say. He's taught me to not battle people's intellects but to win their hearts like Jesus did. I want them to know that God is our heavenly Father and that the Rock of our salvation is Jesus Christ. Not that I demonstrate it perfectly, but I trust that God's grace covers my shortcomings.

Men, let's look for opportunities to share our stories, just as they are, to others, and to point them to our Rock. After all, our stories aren't ours, per se, but are part of *the story* of the One working in us and through us. The words are His, planted in us by His Spirit through all of life's experiences that He has prepared for us. God is the one to transform their hearts of stone to hearts of flesh, dependent on the Rock. It is a marvelous thing to be used by the One who loved us enough to die for us. That others might become His eternal offspring through faith in Christ is bold beyond comparison, just like the Rock that He is.

Men, let's look for opportunities to share our stories, just as they are, to others, and to point them to our Rock.

Prayer: Almighty God, my Father and my Rock, thank You for Your faithfulness and steadfast love You have shown me through Your Son, Jesus Christ. Crush my stubborn pride, and help me to listen as well as speak, so that I might winsomely declare Your saving name. I ask this through Christ, my Lord. Amen.

Friday

DAILY STUDY QUESTIONS
Psalm 89:24-29

1. What was the last song or catchphrase you had stuck in your head? Was it a good thing or a bad thing?

2. How might the song of God's Gospel in Christ be like one of these ditties that get lodged in your head and won't stop?

3. The word *horn* appears often in the Psalms (here in v. 24). What comes to mind when you hear this word?

4. While today's verses from Psalm 89 may not be overly familiar to every reader, they certainly present a memorable and compelling portrait of God's favor for His chosen servant. Which of these blessings conveys the most significance for you?

5. As great as David was, the blessings of verse 27 could apply only to David's greater Son. How does the further promise of verse 29 bring great comfort to us?

PSALM 89

The 89th psalm is a prophecy of Christ and His kingdom. The psalmist calls it a heavenly kingdom (as Christ Himself does in the Gospel). It takes up the prophecy of Christ given to David and emphasizes it with an abundant spirit. Particularly, the psalmist emphasizes that this kingdom shall never, for the sake of any sin, come to an end or be left behind. Accordingly, our salvation shall not be based on our piety, though the promised kingdom of the Jews and all other earthly kingdoms last no longer or stretch no further than they are pious.

But later the psalmist begins to prophesy that such a precious and fruitful kingdom would be trampled, torn, and subverted by the Antichrist, so that it appears as though God has forgotten His former abundant promises and is doing the opposite of His own words. But this all is announced beforehand, to be a comfort to us in these last days. Therefore, we should not despair, though it seems to us that there is no Christendom, no light of the Church, anymore on earth. Yet it always remains, however distressed, broken, and persecuted.

– Martin Luther

GROUP BIBLE STUDY
(Questions and answers on pp.174–76.)

1. What was the best or the worst deal you ever made? Tell the group about what made that deal so remarkable.

2. The common biblical word for a binding agreement is *covenant*. What is the nature of the covenant in Psalm 89:3? What makes this covenant uniquely different from the deals that we make?

3. Given the fact that David's royal lineage did not last beyond a few centuries (the Kingdom of Judah itself did not make it past 586 BC and Israel ended even earlier!), how are we to understand the promise of this eternal covenant (vv. 3–4) made by the faithful Lord?

4. In verse 9, part of the praise of Yahweh includes His control over the sea and its waves, which in the Old Testament consistently represent chaos and evil. Why might the sea be considered an apt symbol for the resting place of evil?

5. Walking 'in the light of [God's] face" is not a phrase Christians often use (v. 15). Describe how it feels when you walk in the light of God's face. What does it look like to others?

6. The basic idea of the Gospel is God Himself intervening for the sake of His creatures. How do verses 16–18 convey a strong Gospel message? Which particular phrases in these verses declare the essence of the Gospel?

7. This psalm, like so many, exults in the privileged position of David, the second king of Israel (vv. 19–29). What made David so special to the Lord? At what point do these words no longer apply merely to David but to David's greater Son?

8. Verse 28 contains one of the most beautiful words in the Old Testament, a Hebrew word that is variously translated "loving-kindness," "mercy," "love," and "steadfast love." What is the source of this loving-kindness, and what does the promise of verse 28 teach us about God?

9. Studying a messianic psalm teaches us more about our God and Savior, but beyond merely supplying head knowledge, what difference does it make for our lives to know that God's messianic plan was gaining momentum already in the time of David?

10. How will your greater appreciation for God's work of preparing the way for His Messiah make a difference in your life this week?

Week Two

Psalm 93

[1] The LORD reigns; He is robed in majesty;
the LORD is robed; He has put on strength as His belt.
Yes, the world is established; it shall never be moved.

[2] Your throne is established from of old;
You are from everlasting.

[3] The floods have lifted up, O LORD,
the floods have lifted up their voice;
the floods lift up their roaring.

[4] Mightier than the thunders of many waters,
mightier than the waves of the sea,
the LORD on high is mighty!

[5] Your decrees are very trustworthy;
holiness befits Your house,
O LORD, forevermore.

Gary Dunker

Psalm 93:1

The Lord reigns; He is robed in majesty; the Lord is robed;
He has put on strength as His belt. Yes, the world is established; it shall never be moved.

The Lord Reigns

Some actors are indistinguishable from their movie roles. For me, Judy Garland is forever Dorothy, Ray Bolger remains the Scarecrow, Jack Haley, the Tin Man, and Bert Lahr, the Cowardly Lion—all in the 1939 movie *The Wizard of Oz*. Of these, my favorite remains Bert Lahr. Perhaps you recall Lahr's portrayal of the Cowardly Lion, who desired to reign as king of the forest, yet he lacked the wherewithal to make it happen. Together with Dorothy, the Tin Man, the Scarecrow, and Toto the dog, he embarked on a quest to find the Wizard of Oz—and found that what he needed most he already possessed.

There is only one scene where we see the Cowardly Lion in his regal splendor. (Personally, I consider this Bert Lahr's best performance in the film.) It occurs during the song "If I Were King of the Forest." For a few brilliant moments, the Cowardly Lion, adorned with a red bow in the top of his mane, feigns bravery. He pompously struts about the stage. His three new friends place a robe about his shoulders. With the swipe of his axe, the Tin Man creates a crown from a flowerpot and places it on the Cowardly Lion's head.

Many psalms, like Psalm 93, describe God's regal splendor. In verse 1, David describes the Lord as He reigns over heaven and earth. Unlike the counterfeit courage of the Cowardly Lion, the psalmist reveals the true King. Psalm 97:1 reminds us that because God reigns we have cause to rejoice, especially as we consider the salvation Christ won for us at Calvary. Psalm 99:1 acknowledges the awesomeness of God's rule: "The Lord reigns; let the peoples tremble!" The psalmist does not describe a pretender to the throne, but the real King, the Creator, Redeemer, and Sanctifier of life. Other passages of Scripture also speak about God's reign as our heavenly

King. The prophet Isaiah wrote, "How beautiful upon the mountains are the feet of him who brings good news, who publishes peace, who brings good news of happiness, who publishes salvation, who says to Zion, 'Your God reigns'" (Isaiah 52:7). In this verse, God's reign as King is seen in His salvation, which is proclaimed and brought about through the proclamation of His Good News. "The LORD reigns" is all Israel's confession; it is our confession as Christians before the world (see Psalm 96:10; 97:1).

The Cowardly Lion's regal robe symbolized his power and authority. When his companions placed the robe about his shoulders and a crown upon his head, they completed his outward transformation. Contrast this with the robbing and crowning of the Lord Jesus: "And the soldiers twisted together a crown of thorns and put it on his head and arrayed him in a purple robe" (John 19:2) Later, on the cross, Christ "robed Himself" with our sins, humbling Himself (Philippians 2:8) that He might clothe us with His righteousness in Baptism (Galatians 3:26–27). Paul expressed it this way, "For our sake He made Him to be sin who knew no sin, so that in Him we might become the righteousness of God" (2 Corinthians 5:21). On earth, Jesus was enthroned on a cross so that we might be enthroned with Him in heaven.

Note, too, that David points out the magnificent strength of God: "The LORD is robed; He has put on strength as a belt." Unlike the Cowardly Lion, our God sits enthroned as the epitome of strength. Job notes that there is none like God, who is so strong He is able to bestow strength on those who are utterly weak: "How You have helped him who has no power! How you have saved the arm that has no strength!" (26:2). God is so strong that He "hangs the earth on nothing" (v. 7). On our own, we have no strength; we're no more powerful than the Cowardly Lion as he pompously strutted about.

My mom always said, "Pay attention when God says the same thing on more than one occasion." I believe her. "The LORD is my strength and my song; He has become my salvation" is repeated in three places in the Bible: Exodus 15:2; Psalm 118:14; and Isaiah 12:2. Moses, David, and Isaiah recognized and affirmed God's strong arm working out their salvation. However, God's strength would do us no good, in fact it would do us eternal harm, were not God *for us*. How blessed we are that in Christ our strong God is for us, not against us (Romans 8:31)! How blessed we are that the Holy Spirit has robed us in God's strength. How blessed we are that Christ feeds us through His Word and His Supper and will do so until the day we see Him face-to-face.

"Yes, the world is established; it shall never be moved" (Psalm 93:1). God established the universe by His Word. In the beginning *with* God and *as* God, our

Savior, the Word, made all things. "Without Him was not any thing made that was made. In Him was life, and the life was the light of men" (John 1:3–4). That same Word that brought creation into existence has brought us new life and light and has made us God's sons through faith in Him. We look forward to the day of His return, when we will join with Him in the air (1 Thessalonians 4:17) to witness the Lord re-creating the heavens and the earth (2 Peter 3:11–13).

In Oz, the wizard awarded the Cowardly Lion a medal for the bravery that he had demonstrated by caring for his friends. On the Last Day, we will be rewarded for the good works we accomplished on earth, not in order to receive salvation, but because salvation was freely given to us through faith in Christ (Ephesians 2:8–10). Because of God's mercy through our Savior, we will join in the hymn of heaven's company, "Worthy is the Lamb who was slain, to receive power and wealth and wisdom and might and honor and glory and blessing" (Revelation 5:12). May God's Spirit strengthen our faith through His Means of Grace. Indeed, what a blessing it is to confess with our own lips, "The Lord reigns, He is robed in majesty; the Lord is robed; He has put on strength as His belt (Psalm 93:1)" Amen.

How blessed we are that Christ feeds us through His Word and His Supper and will do so until the day we see Him face-to-face.

Prayer: Heavenly Father, You are great and majestic, while I am sinful and unworthy. Have mercy on me, O Lord, and cleanse me of all my sins through the blood of Jesus Christ, Your Son, my Lord. Amen.

Monday

DAILY STUDY QUESTIONS
Psalm 93:1

1. What images come to mind when you think of kings?

2. Why is the idea of *king* so readily applicable to God?

3. While God has every right to be named King and Lord—even of your own life—do you always recognize and appreciate His right to rule in your life?

4. What are some of the ways that you become a "royal pretender" and try to be the king of your own life; that is, what are some areas where you especially struggle with allowing God to be the sovereign Ruler of your life?

5. How can the knowledge that the world is firmly established under God's rule provide you with assurance and encouragement as you make your way through the coming day?

Psalm 93:2

Your throne is established from of old;
You are from everlasting.

Old as the Hills

Over the years I've enjoyed several trips to Mount Rushmore in the Black Hills of South Dakota. I remember traveling there for the golden anniversary of my great aunt and uncle, for a Boy Scouts camping trip, and even on my honeymoon. Later, my wife and I took our two daughters to visit this national landmark. In our family, from that point on, Mount Rushmore has carried the nickname my daughters applied to it: "the Faces."

Mount Rushmore is the masterpiece of American sculptor Gutzon Borglum. The four faces of U.S. presidents George Washington, Thomas Jefferson, Teddy Roosevelt, and Abraham Lincoln testify not only to the greatness of the men depicted in granite, but also to the hundreds of men who once swarmed over the mountain, determined to leave their legacy in stone. The Mount Rushmore monument was begun in 1927 and was dedicated in 1941.

In the Black Hills, there is also an area known as "the Needles." These rock formations were originally considered as the place to carve the presidents. Borglum nixed the idea, finding the Needles too fragile. Instead, Borglum's eyes fell on Mount Rushmore, whose granite is said to erode at a rate of one inch every ten thousand years. Some may say that at that rate, "the Faces" carved on Mount Rushmore will last forever. In reality, we have little idea how long Mount Rushmore will survive. Perhaps an earthquake or other natural disaster may one day cause "the Faces" to tumble into ruins. Other human landmarks have met similar fates. We need but think of the Seven Wonders of the Ancient World to be reminded that the works of men do not remain forever.

In Psalm 93:2, the psalmist tells us that God's throne is "from of old," and that He is "from everlasting." Other psalms make this point. For example, Psalm 45:6 reads, "Your throne, O God, is forever and ever." Then in Psalm 89, we find interesting accent about another throne. To David, God says, "I will establish your offspring forever, and build Your throne for all generations" (v. 4), and about God's own throne we read, "Righteousness and justice are the foundation of Your throne" (v. 14). Later, God speaks these words about David, "I will establish his offspring forever and his throne as the days of the heavens" (v. 29). Then in verses 36 and 37, we read, "His [David's] offspring shall endure forever, his throne as long as the sun before Me. Like the moon it shall be established forever, a faithful witness in the skies." The throne of God is eternal. So, too, is the throne of the God-man, the Son of David, our Lord and Savior, Jesus Christ.

Dynamite and hard labor brought "the Faces" into view. From the widest point, the finished sculpture measures some 365 feet across. I remember reading a story suggesting that craftsmen deliberately made George Washington's nose an inch too long, so that it would end up exactly right ten thousand years from now. True or not, we know from Scripture that God's throne will remain forever. Jesus Christ, as the eternal Son of God and the Son of David, sits on this throne. Jesus is the fulfillment of God's promise to David about his throne. Hebrews 1:8 says, "But of the Son He says, 'Your throne, O God, is forever and ever,'" echoing the words of Psalm 45:6. Luke recorded the angel Gabriel's words to Mary: "The Lord God will give to Him the throne of his father David, and He will reign over the house of Jacob forever, and of His kingdom there will be no end" (Luke 1:32–33). What Gabriel promised Mary about her Son echoes what God through Nathan the prophet had promised David: "Your house and your kingdom shall be made sure forever before Me. Your throne shall be established forever" (2 Samuel 7:16). Each dynamite blast and each chisel blow to Mount Rushmore revealed the features of an American president. So, too, does Holy Scripture reveal the features of the world's eternal Redeemer, Jesus Christ.

Mount Rushmore attracts thousands of tourists annually. Rising as a silent beacon of national pride, it stands some 6,200 feet above sea level. For Christians, our silent beacon remains the cross of Mount Calvary. The cross was Christ's earthly throne. As Jesus hung suspended between heaven and earth, God forsook Him. Jesus said, "My God, My God, why have You forsaken Me?" (Matthew 27:46). God placed His wrath and His judgment of sin on Christ instead of us. "[Christ is] waiting from that time until His enemies should be made a footstool for His feet. For by a single offering He has perfected for all time those who are being sanctified" (Hebrews 10:12–14). God's work of salvation, completed in Christ's life, death, and resurrection, is applied to us in His Word and Sacraments. Like a sculptor's hands with a stone, He has perfected us to eternal life through the gift of faith. Now, through the same Means of Grace, He is making us holy. Paul reminds us, "We were buried therefore with Him by Baptism into death, in order that, just as Christ was raised from the dead by the glory of the Father, we too might walk in newness of life" (Romans 6:4). Skillful hands spent nearly twenty years crafting a monument in stone at Mount Rushmore. God crafts those who believe on His Son throughout a lifetime.

Recall the fifth stanza of *Amazing Grace*: "When we've been there ten thousand years, Bright shining as the sun, We've no less days to sing God's praise Than when we'd first begun."

We don't know if the faces of Washington, Jefferson, Roosevelt, and Lincoln will remain ten thousand years from now; none of us will be alive to confirm or deny it. But through God's Word we do know that Jesus' throne will remain forever. May we stay faithful while we wait for Christ's return—either at our death or at His Second Coming—there to live with Him and worship Him on His eternal throne. For, if we confess with our mouth "Jesus is Lord" and believe in our heart that God raised him from the dead, we will be saved (Romans 10:9).

Like stone in a sculptor's hands, He has perfected us to eternal life through the gift of faith. Now, through the same Means of Grace, He is making us holy.

Prayer: Heavenly Father, chip away and remove the sin in my life. By Your Holy Spirit, renew me, so that I may bring glory to You and Your eternal throne forever. I ask this in Jesus' name. Amen.

Tuesday

DAILY STUDY QUESTIONS
Psalm 93:2

1. Mount Rushmore—rather a permanent landmark—was completed in 1941, what is the oldest and most permanent historic landmark you have visited?

2. Some translations follow the Hebrew closely and tell us that God's throne was "established from of old" (v. 2). When, exactly, is "from of old"?

3. The idea of *everlasting* presents severe challenges to us as human beings. How would you define *everlasting*?

4. Long after any troubles in this created world cease to exist, God will still be. How does this reality provide comfort and reassurance for you as you face routine challenges and trials?

5. What difference should it make for the way you live your life when you remember that the everlasting God is *your* God and Father?

Psalm 93:3

The floods have lifted up, O Lord, the floods have lifted up
their voice; the floods lift up their roaring.

His Cleansing Flood

From Pier 33 we gazed north. A mile away, we could make out the buildings of Alcatraz. On this gunmetal gray day, a ferryboat sailed my aunt and uncle and my wife and me away from Fisherman's Wharf. Waves in San Francisco Bay buffeted us from side to side. Yet the ferry's pilot focused only on Alcatraz and our safe harbor one mile away.

In Psalm 93:3, David stirs up an image of seas in revolt. The Lord had brought order out of chaos at creation and placed the seas under His dominion. Moses records, "In the beginning God created the heavens and the earth. The earth was without form and void, and darkness was over the face of the deep. And the Spirit of God was hovering over the face of the waters" (Genesis 1:1–2). Then he adds,

> And God said, "Let there be an expanse in the midst of the waters, and let it separate the waters from the waters." And God made the expanse and separated the waters that were under the expanse from the waters that were above the expanse. And it was so. And God called the expanse Heaven. And there was evening and there was morning, the second day. And God said, "Let the waters under the heavens be gathered together into one place, and let the dry land appear." And it was so. God called the dry land Earth, and the waters that were gathered together He called Seas. And God saw that it was good. (Genesis 1:6–10)

Everything we read in Genesis 1 presents creation as God intended.

As our tiny boat pressed on toward Alcatraz, I couldn't help but recall how Adam and Eve's rebellion changed God's perfect creation. In one brief moment in time, the world God created with His all-powerful Word was placed under His curse. God rushed to Adam and said, "Cursed is the ground because of you" (Genesis

3:17). This curse of sin affects not only the "ground" but the seas as well. All of God's creation groans. Natural disasters such as earthquakes, tsunamis, hurricanes, and tornadoes bear witness to a world cursed by God because of man's sin.

Another boat comes to mind—the ark Noah built. It, too, found itself tossed about on sin-caused hostile seas. "Now the earth was corrupt in God's sight, and the earth was filled with violence. And God saw the earth, and behold, it was corrupt, for all flesh had corrupted their way on the earth" (Genesis 6:11–13). In all, God saved eight people—Noah and his wife, and their three sons and three daughters-in-law. "They went into the ark with Noah, two and two of all flesh in which there was the breath of life. And those that entered, male and female of all flesh, went in as God had commanded him. And the LORD shut him in" (Genesis 7:15–16). The last six words of verse 16 have always stuck with me—"And the LORD shut him in." God sealed Noah and his tiny family into the ark. God protected them although the waters rose to horrific heights, washing sin from the face of the earth. As a reminder of His grace to Noah and all generations to follow, God put a rainbow in the sky, saying, "This is the sign of the covenant that I make between me and you and every living creature that is with you, for all future generations" (Genesis 9:12).

I am not saying that the seas that day in San Francisco Bay reached epic proportions. They didn't. Nevertheless, as water sprayed over us on this overcast day, I couldn't help thinking about how Noah and his family might have felt that day so long ago. Then, I thought about me again. Don't I feel crushed by the world around me at times (and I'm sure I'm not alone)? A loss of a job, a wayward child, a downturn in the economy, watching our 401Ks melting away, or even the return of a sin I thought I had under control, all these can bring about the crushing wave of despair. David felt it, too. He recorded his thoughts this way: "The cords of death entangled me; the torrents of destruction overwhelmed me" (Psalm 18:4). At these times, we find it easy to forget that the hand on the rudder of our ship of life belongs to none other than God, our heavenly Father, our Creator and Redeemer.

And yet, as God saved Noah, He has also saved us. God made Jesus' death and resurrection ours in a saving flood. Peter tells us,

> For Christ also suffered once for sins, the righteous for the unrighteous, that He might bring us to God, being put to death in the flesh but made alive in the spirit, in which He went and proclaimed to the spirits in prison, because they formerly did not obey, when God's patience waited in the days of Noah, while the ark was being prepared, in which a few, that is, eight persons, were brought safely through the water.

Baptism, which corresponds to this, now saves you, not as a removal of dirt from the body but as an appeal to God for a good conscience, through the resurrection of Jesus Christ, who has gone to heaven and is at the right hand of God, with angels, authorities, and powers having been subjected to Him. (1 Peter 3:18–22)

At last, our ferry docked at Alcatraz. After a few moments ashore, I regained my equilibrium. Sea gulls screamed their "Mine! Mine!" overhead as our party began the ascent to Alcatraz where criminals like Al Capone and "Machine Gun" Kelly once lived behind bars. Sin is our Alcatraz. It keeps us from God as easily as the one mile of San Francisco Bay kept prisoners firmly on Alcatraz Island. Thank God for His work in our Baptism. In Baptism, Jesus Christ grants through water and Word a "good conscience" (1 Peter 3:21). Many times in our lives we may notice how "the floods have lifted up their voice" (Psalm 93:3), but we can always remember our Baptism and feel secure again in God's hands.

....

And yet, as God saved Noah, He has also saved us. God made Jesus' death and resurrection ours in a saving flood.

Prayer: Lord Jesus Christ, Your Word stilled both wind and wave. Speak Your Word of peace into the tempestuous seas of my heart and cause me to rejoice in Your cleansing flood. I ask in Your name. Amen.

....

Wednesday

DAILY STUDY QUESTIONS
Psalm 93:3

1. What is the most frightening experience you have had on the water?

2. Why is it that the pounding of surf, the thundering of a waterfall, and the roaring of a flood can be such terrifying sounds?

3. God brought the waters under submission on the second day of creation. How does this truth combat ideas of an eternal battle between "good" and "evil"?

4. To what extent has the rebellion of creation thwarted God's original plan? In other words, how broken is creation?

5. What inroads of the rebellion of evil will you strive to resist and overcome in the coming day?

Mightier than the thunders of many waters, mightier than
the waves of the sea, the LORD on high is mighty!

Mightier Than the Waters

I have my daughter's permission to share the following story:

Emotions rushed over me in waves. Disbelief, yes, and, I admit, even anger at God. *Lord, what have I done to deserve this?* I thought. I reeled from the blow. *My daughter is pregnant, she's not married, and there's no boyfriend in sight. This can't be happening. After all, she went to Lutheran schools.* Don't misunderstand me, I know that emotional trials come to Christians and non-Christians alike, but this trial hit home. My twenty-two-year-old daughter now carried my first grandchild.

Psalm 93:4 addresses times of emotional chaos. Indeed, there are times in all of our lives when we hear the "thunders of many waters" as David so aptly describes the roar of the deep. David knew all about "many waters" in his life. Think of his extramarital affair. While David's army headed off to war, he stayed behind. One night, David got out of bed to walk around the roof of his palace. Looking down, his gaze fell upon a woman as she bathed. It didn't take long before David knew her name: Bathsheba, the wife of Uriah, a member of David's royal guard. Quickly, David dispatched a messenger to bring Bathsheba. He slept with her—a one-night stand with incredible consequences. It wasn't long before a messenger arrived at the palace with news for David (probably stunning him as much as my daughter's words stunned me). The messenger brought only three words: "I am pregnant" (2 Samuel 11:5).

Loving someone who disappoints us is difficult. I know, I've been there. *I want you out of my house!* passed through my mind. Almost as quickly came the words, *What if God kicked you out every time you sinned?* Then my mind carried me back to the first time I held my daughter. I could hear anew the doctor's call to put her down and get out of the room. My wife suffered complications during delivery. I held my firstborn—a new life—while my wife's life slipped away. She recovered, but my daughter has always held a special place in my heart because of this event. I saw this baby again when I looked into my daughter's eyes that night.

God used the prophet Nathan to teach David about forgiveness, just as He used the memory of my daughter's birth to teach me. David cried out to Nathan's rebuke, "I have sinned against the LORD" (2 Samuel 12:13). In Psalm 51, David pours out his heart to God for his sin of adultery: "Have mercy on me, O God, according to Your steadfast love; according to Your abundant mercy blot out my transgressions. Wash me thoroughly from all my iniquity, and cleanse me from my sin!" (vv. 1–2). And later, "Create in me a clean heart, O God, and renew a right spirit within me. Cast me not away from Your presence, and take not Your Holy Spirit from me. Restore to me the joy of Your salvation, and uphold me with a willing spirit" (vv. 10–12). To David's plea for mercy, Nathan replied on God's behalf, "The LORD also has put away your sin" (2 Samuel 12:13).

David's great confession and Nathan's absolution point us to Christ. So does Psalm 93:4. David's sin with Bathsheba caused "many waters" to break over his life. Our sins do the same. Yet, as David points out in our psalm, God is "mightier than the thunders of many waters, mightier than the waves of the sea." God foreknew our sinful natures and sent His own child as our Redeemer. Isaiah puts it this way, "For to us a child is born, to us a son is given and the government shall be on His shoulder, and His name shall be called Wonderful Counselor, Mighty God, Everlasting Father, Prince of Peace. Of the increase of His government and of peace there will be no end" (Isaiah 9:6–7).

If God forgave David in his sin, and if Jesus forgave the world from the cross saying, "Father, forgive them, for they know not what they do" (Luke 23:34), then how could I not forgive my daughter? Some may ask, "How could you insist that your daughter have this child?" Those who offer such words have failed to read Psalm 127:3, "Children are a heritage from the LORD, the fruit of the womb a reward." Children are not a punishment but a reward.

My grandson turned six this year. This fall his mother moved out of our home to begin a teaching career. My grandson moved with her. God certainly played a significant role in restoring a once-broken relationship. I imagine that some may read this devotional and say, "Regardless of the situation, I'm a man. I can handle it." I say truthfully, "I couldn't!" Frankly, King David couldn't either. That is why he penned this bit of advice, "Great is our LORD, and abundant in power; His understanding is beyond measure" (Psalm 147:5). God knows us intimately. His understanding exceeds ours.

In the Fifth Petition of the Lord's Prayer, Christ calls upon us to seek the Lord's forgiveness while we forgive those who sin against us. You remember the words "Forgive us our debts, as we also have forgiven our debtors" (Matthew 6:12). Nowhere do we see God's triumph over "many waters" clearer than in the forgiveness of sin. Through the death and resurrection of His Son, He proves "mightier than the thunders of many waters, mightier than the waves of the sea—the Lord on high is mighty!" (Psalm 93:4). He who created us, also saw us in our sin and redeemed us. I take comfort in 1 John 1:9, "If we confess our sins, he is faithful and just to forgive us our sins and to cleanse us from all unrighteousness." I pray that as you face "many waters" in life, you will turn your face to the "Lord on high." I'm learning forgiveness by His hand as He calms my life's sometimes troubled seas.

In the Fifth Petition of the Lord's Prayer, Christ calls upon us to seek the Lord's forgiveness while we forgive those who sin against us.

Prayer: O Lord God, You are indeed mightier than many waters. When I am in trouble, help me to cling to You and the sure footing You have given me through Your Son, Jesus Christ, my Lord. In His name I pray. Amen.

Thursday

DAILY STUDY QUESTIONS
Psalm 93:4

1. When was a time you experienced a situation that seriously challenged your ability to forgive?

2. How can remembering biblical stories of astounding grace and forgiveness enable us to extend forgiveness?

3. What makes the astounding way that God delivers grace and forgives sins one of the greatest demonstrations of His power over the chaos of evil?

4. What images come to mind when you think of the "Lord on high"?

5. How can being armed with divine forgiveness enable you to live in a more godlike way in the day ahead?

Psalm 93:5

Your decrees are very trustworthy; holiness befits Your
house, O Lord, forevermore.

Forevermore

I can relate to the expression "forevermore." The days between the ages of ten and sixteen seemed like forever to me. I wanted to drive a car but wasn't old enough. I watched as others I knew got their driver's licenses and drove. But me? I was stuck riding a bicycle. My younger daughter once said that she was "four for forty-hundred years." I thought that about my fifteenth year. That year, I drove with adults present but never soloed. Finally, the time arrived to receive my driver's license. To my horror, I received a driver's manual instead of the keys to my father's car. Do you remember your first driver's manual filled with rules and regulations governing how to drive motor vehicles? These rules and regulations served to protect drivers and pedestrians alike. Know the rules, pass the test, and drive the car.

For drivers, driver's manuals provide decrees (statutes or laws) for safe driving. Decrees such as to signal your turns, obey the speed limit, don't pass in a no-passing zone, and others. God has decrees too. David directs our attention to God's decrees in Psalm 93:5, pointing out that God's "decrees are very trustworthy." In other words, David reminds us that God's decrees remain rock-solid. Unlike man's laws, which may change over time, God's decrees never change. In the Psalms, David often speaks about God's decrees. In an earlier psalm, David notes,

The law of the Lord is perfect, reviving the soul; the testimony of the Lord is sure, making wise the simple; the precepts of the Lord are right, rejoicing the heart; the commandment of the Lord is pure, enlightening the eyes; the fear of the Lord is clean, enduring forever; the rules of the Lord are true, and righteous altogether. More to be desired are they than gold, even much fine gold; sweeter also than honey and drippings off the honeycomb. Moreover, by them is Your servant warned; in keeping them there is great reward. (Psalm 19:7–11)

I could not drive a motor vehicle alone until I reached the age of sixteen and passed both written and driving examinations. Nebraska reinforced these laws with penalties for breaking them. God's Law, as David noted earlier, warns us and rewards us. It warns us that a stiff penalty accompanies sinning against them. While sinning against driving regulations may result in fines, jail time, or even the forfeiture of our driver's license, sinning against God's decrees results in death. God's clarion warning pronounces, "The wages of sin is death" (Romans 6:23). Our sinfulness merits the death sentence. James puts it this way, "Then desire when it has conceived gives birth to sin, and sin when it is fully grown brings forth death" (James 1:15).

David speaks further about God's decrees in Psalm 119: "Your [God's] testimonies are righteous forever; give me understanding that I may live" (Psalm 119:144). Although sin prevents us from keeping God's testimonies, or statutes, perfectly, God's grace in Christ grants us eternal life and the desire to keep them. From God's hand, we do not receive the death that our many sins merit. Instead, we receive eternal life. Because our relationship with God has been sealed with Christ's blood, and because Christ kept God's statutes perfectly for us, we are set free. We are set free from the condemnation of the Law and set free to delight in it. By the Spirit's power working through the Gospel, we hunger for God to impart His wisdom to us through His Word.

God's decrees also speak about faith granted by His Spirit. The Holy Spirit helps us understand the exclusivity of Christ's words in John 14:6, when He says, "I am the way, and the truth, and the life. No one comes to the Father except through me." We may find those who speak against such exclusivity, saying that all religions point to the same god. Against this point of view, God's Word stands firm. Leaning not on our own understanding, but on God's "very trustworthy" words, we believe what Jesus says about Himself: "I am the door. If anyone enters by Me, he will be saved" (John 10:9).

Trusting in God's deliverance, in His strength and salvation, David writes, "I love You, O Lord, my strength. The Lord is my rock and my fortress and my deliverer, my God, my rock, in whom I take refuge, my shield, and the horn of my salvation, my stronghold" (Psalm 18:1–2). Later in this same psalm, David writes, "The Lord lives, and blessed be my rock, and exalted be the God of my salvation" (v. 46). David knows and understands whom to credit for his salvation: the Messiah, Jesus Christ, God's Word made flesh (John 1:14). Jesus is David's Son, but Jesus is also David's Rock, Fortress, Deliverer, and Savior.

It seemed like it took forever to receive my driver's license. Now, forty-one years later, time doesn't seem to move so slowly. While the decrees of man provide security for the road, God's decrees provide security with a heaven-bound guarantee. God's decrees "are very trustworthy." As heads of households, we men carry the responsibility to educate our children in God's decrees. Led by God's grace through the Holy Spirit, we "train up a child in the way he should go," receiving in return God's guarantee that "even when he is old he will not depart from it" (Proverbs 22:6).

David knows and understands whom to credit for his salvation: the Messiah, Jesus Christ, God's Word made flesh (John 1:14).

Prayer: Dear Holy Spirit, through Your Word show me my sins and point me to the cross of my Savior. Help me to delight in God's decrees and to apply them diligently to my life. In Jesus' name. Amen.

Friday

DAILY STUDY QUESTIONS
Psalm 93:5

1. What's good and what's bad about having to wait to fulfill the letter of the Law?

2. The psalmist asserts that God's testimonies (in other words, God's Law) are fully confirmed. How have you experienced the veracity of God's Law and confirmed those laws in your own life?

3. This final verse of the psalm seems to introduce a rather abrupt change of subject. What connection might there be between this verse and the previous four?

4. As a son of God, you are a member of God's household. What is God's expectation for the way that you are to live?

5. What decrees of God need your special attention as you face your present opportunities and challenges?

Week Two

PSALM 93

....

The 93rd psalm is a prophecy of the kingdom
of Christ, that it is as wide as the world and
remains forever. Although floods and waters
storm against it, that is, the world's death
and rage oppose and struggle against it, they
accomplish nothing at all; for He is greater
than the world and its prince. This kingdom and
all things will be ordered through His Word,
without sword or armor. He will adorn
His house and make it holy. For the true
worship that adorns and illuminates this house
is preaching, praise, and thanksgiving, which
belong to neither Moses nor the Old Testament.

—Martin Luther

GROUP BIBLE STUDY
(Questions and answers on pp. 180–82.)

1. Living in a democracy, there is sometimes a debate about who is actually in charge. Share with the group your opinion about who really has the power in this country.

2. Why do you think that even people without a sovereign ruler as a figurehead are still interested in the idea of royalty? What is it about royalty that is so fascinating and perhaps even attractive to most people?

3. The first verse seems to make an abrupt change from praising God's majesty to celebrating the foundation and certainty of the created realm. Is there a way that the two thoughts might actually be related?

4. What evidence do you see that would challenge the claim that the world is firmly established? On the other hand, what evidence might you offer in support of the claim?

5. What is the relationship between God's throne being established from of old and His very essence being everlasting? Which came first?

OKAY TO COPY THIS PAGE.   64

6. Some contend that thinking about God's character and attributes is little more than an academic exercise void of any relevance to real life. What possible real life applications might one make from the inconceivable reality that God is everlasting?

7. The psalmist uses the technique of personification, giving the floods a voice. What do you think the flood was doing with its voice? What does the psalmist gain by using this technique?

8. How does an ocean whipped into a frenzy by a storm or a mighty flood sweeping away all in its path provide an apt picture of the rule and action of sin and evil in our lives? What is it about sin that feels like a flood that will not be stopped? Finally, what does this image have to do with God's majesty?

9. The devotion for Thursday connected God's mighty acts with His action of forgiving sin. How does this move substantiate the old adage that to err is human but to forgive is divine?

10. What specific actions will you take in the next week to live like one who is a child of the king, conformed to the king's testimonies?

Week Three

Psalm 101

¹ I will sing of steadfast love and justice;
to You, O Lord, I will make music.

² I will ponder the way that is blameless.
Oh when will You come to me?
I will walk with integrity of heart
within my house;

³ I will not set before my eyes
anything that is worthless.
I hate the work of those who fall away;
it shall not cling to me.

⁴ A perverse heart shall be far from me;
I will know nothing of evil.

⁵ Whoever slanders his neighbor secretly
I will destroy.
Whoever has a haughty look and an arrogant heart
I will not endure.

⁶ I will look with favor on the faithful in the land,
that they may dwell with me;
he who walks in the way that is blameless
shall minister to me.

⁷ No one who practices deceit
shall dwell in my house;
no one who utters lies
shall continue before my eyes.

⁸ Morning by morning I will destroy
all the wicked in the land,
cutting off all the evildoers
from the city of the Lord.

Charles Strohacker

Psalm 101:1

I will sing of steadfast love and justice; to You, O Lord, I will make music.

Don't Just Move Your Lips

Uh-oh. As is usually the case, I am in trouble from the outset. Just three words into the text above and I have failed. And again, near the end, just in case I missed it the first time, the point is driven home. *Sing.* You see, I can't sing. I was diagnosed with my inability at an early age. Standing in the choir loft one afternoon practicing with my class, our fifth-grade teacher broke the news to me: "Chuck, when we sing for church this Sunday, maybe you should just move your lips." She may have also mentioned something about gum, or perhaps it was peanuts. I can't recall exactly.

Now, take it easy. Don't get all upset with my fifth-grade teacher. I loved her dearly for many reasons, and I could go on for pages about the joys I experienced in her class for two years. Hey, it was a double-grade classroom! An inability to sing doesn't necessarily make you a poor student. I enjoyed her beautiful handwriting on the chalkboard, the way she taught grammar, her creative art lessons, and that several days a week when we returned from lunch, she would begin by having us take out our *Golden Book of Songs* and start the afternoon with singing. You see, it isn't that I don't like singing. I love singing, but I was more of a Psalm 100 guy: "Make a joyful noise to the Lord." Joyful shouting—that was me.

Yes, yes, I know, my teacher probably should not have said what she did about my singing exactly that way. I didn't say she was perfect. Maybe it was inexperience or a bad day (although her tone was neither angry nor frustrated), perhaps she had a lot on her mind or words may have simply escaped her. Have words ever escaped you? Not in the sense we usually mean, that you couldn't think of what to say, but rather something slipped out that you wish had remained unsaid or that you wish you would have phrased differently. Most likely this is what happened that afternoon. And she was correct. After all, you haven't heard me sing. Or my mom and dad for that matter. Obviously, it's a hereditary thing.

Being unable to sing isn't the worst thing, although I have always felt it to be a personal shortcoming for me as a Lutheran teacher. I truly appreciated the wonderful, powerful singing voices of my pastors and teachers and wish I possessed that gift. An inability to sing is not a sin, although an inability to do anything is certainly a result of sin in our world. In a perfect world, we could do all things, but in a sinful world, we always fall short of God's glory.

I don't know how Adam and Eve sang after the fall into sin, but I'm quite sure that prior to the fall they sang beautifully. Before sin entered the world, everything was perfect, so I would have to assume that included their singing.

What are you unable to do? What are those things that, no matter how hard you try, you fall short in or are unable to accomplish as well as you would like? You love your kids, but let's face it, you are not always the best at parenting. You strive to be a better spouse, neighbor, or co-worker, but for whatever reasons, you fail. Maybe words have escaped you that you wish could be called back. Lack of patience, not enough time, fatigue, stress—all of these things are the result of sin in our world. And due to our sinful hearts, any of them could lead us into temptation.

Of course, some of our sins are obvious and willful. I just plain don't like the neighbor across the street or the guy in the cubicle next to me. Or as in King David's case, perhaps I want something that belongs to someone else. Yes, even David who wrote beautiful psalms and sang with the harp for Saul, well, he had his moments when he sinned and fell short of God's glory.

Psalm 101 is a king's pledge to reign righteously and may even have been written by David for his son Solomon, perhaps when Solomon ascended to the throne as king. But even great kings like David and Solomon break their pledges and need to call on God for His divine forgiveness. Only Jesus, David's heir and a successor in the kingly line, has fulfilled this king's pledge perfectly and, in so doing, has secured for us forgiveness and righteousness in God's sight.

Through Christ, our Savior, salvation is not dependent upon anything we do, our singing, or any other abilities for that matter. Psalm 101 begins, "I will sing of steadfast love and justice." Forgiveness and our salvation begin with God's love, and the psalmist recognizes God's love at the very beginning of his pledge. He also recognizes God's justice, that part of God that could not allow the penalty or debt of sin to go unpaid.

God reigns as our perfect King, the only one who can rule without error, who dispenses both love and justice perfectly, and who fulfills His pledge of love with faithfulness.

While all earthly pledges inevitably fail, those of kings as well as those of lesser individuals like us, God's pledge endures forever because God is faithful, and His love and justice are perfect. God guarantees His pledge to us through Jesus, things like faithfulness to all generations and steadfast love forever, things which are not dependent on our abilities or made void by our inabilities, even our most willful sin.

God's pledge, His covenant and promise, are not dependent on David's beautiful singing or my monotone, flat, off-key drone. God demonstrated His love for us in His Son, Jesus, and sealed His pledge of love forever with Jesus' precious blood on the cross.

God reigns as our perfect King, the only one who can rule without error, who dispenses both love and justice perfectly, and who fulfills His pledge of love with faithfulness.

Prayer: Heavenly Father, often I think too highly of my abilities or beat myself or others down for not meeting my expectations. Reign in my pride, Lord, and help me to delight in the gifts You have given me and other people. In Jesus' name. Amen.

Monday

DAILY STUDY QUESTIONS
Psalm 101:1

1. What was the most inspiring and memorable singing experience that you have had?

2. What makes singing so special, or in other words, why didn't David just stick to speaking of God's steadfast love and justice?

3. If you were to pick a tune or a style of music, what would you choose for God's steadfast love? What style would you choose for God's justice?

4. What is the relationship between steadfast love and justice? Are they antithetical terms, or can they somehow correlate?

5. What will you do in the coming day to sing praises to the Lord?

Psalm 101:2-4

I will ponder the way that is blameless. Oh when will You come to me? I will walk with integrity of heart within my house. I will not set before my eyes anything that is worthless. I hate the work of those who fall away; it shall not cling to me. A perverse heart shall be far from me; I will know nothing of evil.

A Impenetrable House

The king's pledge continues today, accompanied by a plea to God: "When will You come to me?" He recognizes that God wants us to be "blameless." God doesn't call us to lead a balanced life, although balance in our lives is a popular topic and can at times be healthy, and He doesn't want us to be middle of the road. God wants us way over to one side—blameless.

Once again the king pledges himself to a standard that only God can attain and for which we strive only through God's grace and mercy. God in His perfect love and justice requires a blameless life, and we only approach that through the power of the Holy Spirit and Jesus' precious blood. Only Jesus has lived a blameless life, and through His sacrifice on the cross for our sins, we stand before God forgiven, washed in His blood and blameless in His sight.

Blameless in his work of governing and blameless in his own house are what the psalmist writes about—what a tall order! How are you doing in those two areas of your life? Are you blameless at work, in your relationships with co-workers? What about your family; are you blameless at home?

In order to maintain a blameless heart, the king says he will not look at vile things, he will stay far away from faithless and perverse men, and he will have nothing to do with evil deeds or the people who do such evil. Sounds like avoiding temptation. Great advice, but how do I go about implementing that in my life? Evil is all around me, and because of my sinfulness, it has been within me since birth! Eyes and heart appear to be key to the psalmist.

Our first house, a teacherage in a rural community, sat next to the school and in front of a large field. One morning the phone rang at school, and it was my wife frantically asking if I could come home for a minute. It was about a forty-foot commute, and when I got there she showed me a mouse sitting in the bottom of an empty thirty-gallon trash can in our basement. He somehow had fallen into it and was now standing on his back legs, looking up at me. I picked up the trash can and carried it up the basement stairs, out the back door, across the playground, and to the sugar beet field out back. I returned a few minutes later and replaced the empty trash can in the basement.

"What did you do to the mouse?"

"Do to?" I knew the answer Diane wanted to hear, but the little fellow had looked up at me, eyeball to eyeball. "I turned the trash can over and let him go into the beet field."

Obviously this was neither a correct nor an acceptable answer.

We lived in that house for eight years and only had mice once or twice, depending on how you count. Twice if you count how many times I actually had to remove a mouse from the house. Once if you count the number of different mice that were captured.

Yes, the same mouse was back in the basement the next morning. This time our cat caught it, and I learned an important lesson about what cats do with their prizes—they lay them at the master's feet. In this case, unfortunately, that was Diane. The cat was fast though and very quickly caught the mouse again. I managed to gather up cat and mouse, get them outside and separated, and once again deposit the mouse back in the beet field. After this second "catch and release," however, I inspected all around the house. Where the dryer vent came through the brick wall near the foundation, I found the tiniest bit of mortar missing. I could see light from the basement through this crevice, and I quickly patched that hole. No more mice for as long as we lived there.

The psalmist is going to be on guard; he won't look at vile things or associate with faithless men, and he will stay away from evil. No cracks in his foundation. Scripture tells us, "Out of the heart come evil thoughts, murder, adultery, sexual immorality, theft, false testimony, slander" (Matthew 15:19). The eye can be an excellent partner to the heart, providing an entry point by which additional evil thoughts may gain access and make their way into our heart.

The tiniest hole had allowed a mouse entry into our home years ago. After he was removed and the hole patched, we found several drawers where the mouse had shredded paper or cloth to nest, and bags of seed that he had burrowed into, and well, you know the rest. The mouse had been there a while and had made himself at home in our home. A little bitty mouse and an almost imperceptible hole, but what a huge mess he made once he got inside.

How often have leaders in places of power and authority been brought down by the desires of their heart, desires that perhaps began quite small with something they saw? The eyes looked at something sinful, giving it access to the heart, and oh, what a tragic mess it created: coveting, lying, stealing, adultery, and the like.

I wonder if the king anticipated that he could not live up to his promise of being blameless and of not associating with evil men. He definitely had the correct idea, to stay away from and flee from all evil, but at the beginning of today's text (v. 2), he interjects, "When will You come to me?"

God has come to us in Christ Jesus our Lord, and through Him we have forgiveness of sins. Like the king, we by our own strength cannot completely resist sin. Only by the power of the Spirit do we accomplish the good that we do, and only by the blood of Jesus are we forgiven for those times when we fail.

May our prayer be "Come quickly to me, Lord Jesus. I desire and pledge to keep myself blameless, to guard my eyes and my heart. But Lord, my sin is always before me. Create in me daily a clean heart, O God. Forgive me and renew a right spirit within me for Jesus' sake." Amen.

> Only by the power of the Spirit do we accomplish the good that we do, and only by the blood of Jesus are we forgiven for those times when we fail.

> *Prayer: O Lord God, help me to be blameless in Your sight. Guard the doors of my eyes, lips, ears, and heart and grant me the courage to resist temptation. Thank You for the power of Your Word, which cleanses me from all sin and by which Your Son defeated the devil. In Jesus' name. Amen.*

Tuesday

DAILY STUDY QUESTIONS
Psalm 101:2-4

1. What are the recurrent pests that give you the most trouble?

2. What openings into your heart and life are consistently being exploited to trip you with temptation and drag you into sin?

3. The three verses offer several specific ways that a man can do battle with evil. List the ways suggested by the psalmist, David.

4. Considering David's list of suggested tools for living an upright and God-pleasing life, which area could use some special attention from you right now?

5. God's expectations for His creatures are high! We all need Him to come to us with His grace and forgiveness. David wondered, "When will You come to me?" (v. 2). How would God answer that question if you were asking?

Psalm 101:5

Whoever slanders his neighbor secretly I will destroy.
Whoever has a haughty look and an arrogant heart I will
not endure.

You're In

I really struggled with this verse. So much Law it seems! How will I ever find the Gospel in this text? As we have seen in the previous four verses, the king sets a high standard for himself, one which none of us can ever achieve on our own, but we also learned of God's grace and mercy toward us through Christ our Lord. I fail to live up to the king's pledge, but God in His mercy forgives me. I fall, but God lifts me up.

What I hear above, however, is "You're out!" I live with two wonderful women, my wife and our college-aged daughter. And I admit that they compel me at times to watch a popular fashion show on cable TV. Go ahead and laugh at me. Each week, a group of fashion designers compete on a specific clothing challenge, and at the end of the show, judges decide who will stay and who is eliminated. The show always culminates with a supermodel hostess reciting a list of failures to the two designers who performed most poorly for that particular challenge. They stand before her in a moment of tense silence, dissonant music plays, the camera captures facial close-ups, and with a slight German accent the hostess utters these fateful words to the loser: "You're out!"

I kept getting that "You're out!" feeling as I read and reread today's text, imagining myself standing before God, all my sins exposed, and then being banished from the kingdom. "You're out." What a terrible sensation, but this is exactly how the Law makes us feel when we are confronted.

The words of this text, however, are not God's words of elimination spoken toward me. These are the king's words regarding his court. The king is speaking about behavior that he will not tolerate in his court, and these words are meant to reassure me that God, too, will provide structure to society to maintain order. He will protect His people, me included, by not allowing those who may harm others, the slanderers and the proud, to remain in His court.

Most of us are not like a king—at the top of the ladder with everyone else under us and our authority. Perhaps some of us are at the bottom of the ladder, and everyone appears to be over us. Many are somewhere in between, supervising some who work under our authority while also answering to those in power above us.

I have been blessed to work with what many of us call, for lack of better words, "good bosses," people who treated me with respect, taught me, and, as best they could, protected me from those who would try to do me harm. As a school principal, I pray that I have also fulfilled that role faithfully and to the best of my abilities for students, staff, teachers, and parents.

One of my best bosses was Ray, shop foreman and head of Shipping and Receiving. He was neither at the top (there were vice presidents and the president of the company literally and figuratively above him on the second floor), nor was he at the bottom (that would have been me, cleaning wastebaskets in the basement and doing every sort of dirty job that could only be given to a nonunion high school kid).

Ray was not "king," so he did not have the power to rid our shop kingdom of those who did harm, but he did supervise this domain to the extent that he could keep the mischief in check. The true "king," the owner of the company, was my mother's brother, and he had left orders that his nephew receive no special treatment when he came to work. To Ray, that meant "no special favors for me." A good idea—don't needlessly make others jealous. To those who were like the psalmist describes in the text, however, it meant something way at the other end of the spectrum—open season on the new kid.

For the most part, everyone was pretty good, but there were a few, there always are—several envied Ray or others their positions of authority or perhaps disliked me because I was the owner's nephew, and they occasionally caused some sort of trouble. They usually were not very hardworking, they were the ones who never pitched in for doughnuts yet always ate more than their share, when things went wrong they blamed others, they often tried to get out of work, and they frequently sought opportunities to make others look bad or talk behind their backs. If they had been in King David's court, it sounds like he may have cleared them out quickly, but we don't always have that option.

Have you ever worked with people like that? Have you ever been one of those people?

Maybe it is a good thing that most of us don't hold the same authority as a king. As uneasy as today's text made me feel about standing before the king's judgment seat, I was also overwhelmed imagining the awesome responsibility of wielding such power and authority. The power to say, "You're out!" Have you ever thought of this when you considered your "bosses" and their roles and responsibilities?

It might be tempting to think, "If only I were in charge, things would . . . " How might things be better if you were in charge? More policies? A longer list of rules? Is there someone you would fire? How often isn't "more law" our answer to whatever situation we are trying to put right?

When God chose to make things right, He did not send more commandments; the Pharisees had already done that by adding to them. Rather, God sent His Son. God didn't send rules to make sinners right with Him, but He sent His Son to obey God's rules perfectly for us and to deal with us in justice and love. Christ's sacrifice on the cross covers all our failures. All of them! And now that we're baptized into Him, He does not say that we're out; He says, "You're in!" We pray that God continues to send His Spirit to enable us to deal in this same manner with our family, friends, neighbors, and co-workers.

．．

When God chose to make things right, He did not send more commandments; the Pharisees had already done that by adding to them. Rather, God sent His Son.

Prayer: Almighty God, You have dealt righteously and justly with me, although I do not deserve it. Grant me Your Holy Spirit so that I am able to deal in the same manner with my family, friends, neighbors, and co-workers. I ask this in Jesus' name. Amen.

．．

Wednesday

DAILY STUDY QUESTIONS
Psalm 101:5

1. Recall a time when you were embroiled in a mess caused by someone's slander. What made the situation so difficult and frustrating?

2. Why would David react so strongly and so negatively (the NASB translates: "him I will destroy"!) to the threat of a slanderer in his presence?

3. How is one who slanders related to the person described in the second half of verse 5?

4. People often have a dismissive attitude about the significance of their words. What does this verse say about the importance of our words?

5. Think now about what you will do today if you find yourself in the presence of one who is speaking slander.

Psalm 101:6

I will look with favor on the faithful in the land, that they
may dwell with me; he who walks in the way that is blameless
shall minister to me.

A Blameless Way

This king who pledges to rule righteously (Psalm 101:1) lays out a plan. He will walk blamelessly (vv. 2–4). Yeah, right! Blameless? Next, he will not look at vile things or associate with evil or those who do evil (vv. 2–4). Well, we'll see, . . . Then he will clear his court of the gossips and the slanderers (v. 5). Okay, he is the king, so maybe he can accomplish that last task.

In today's text, the king is only going to recruit the faithful and blameless into his service. Where does this guy live that he can find such people?

Are you in a position where you have the authority and responsibility to hire people? How has it been going in your recruitment of only the faithful and the blameless? If you and I live in the same imperfect and sinful world as the king did, we already know that we are only going to find sinners, like ourselves, to hire. So what is the king talking about?

I believe he is talking about surrounding himself with "good" people in the sense that we as Christians understand this term. We know that "there is not a righteous man on earth who does good and never sins" (Ecclesiastes 7:20). The king has used the word *blameless* before, regarding his personal walk, but he knows that walk is not possible apart from God's power and forgiveness. It will be the same for the people he seeks to serve in his courts. He will look for good and faithful people who, like him, walk blamelessly by the grace of God and through His forgiveness.

A professor in a postgraduate class on leadership once asked us, "Would you hire Lee Iacocca to be the superintendent of your school district?" At the time, Iacocca was CEO of Chrysler Corporation and had just rescued that company from bankruptcy. Iacocca had turned Chrysler around.

Almost unanimously, the answer was "No, he's not an educator." A couple of seasoned administrators disagreed, however, and said that they would be comfortable hiring the auto executive because of his extraordinary leadership skills.

The professor's conclusion was that he also would hire Iacocca to run his school district. Why? Because he wasn't hiring this executive to teach children, he was hiring him to lead an organization. "After all," he speculated, "do you think Lee Iacocca can assemble a car?" Probably not. Most likely, the Chrysler CEO surrounded himself with people who knew all the various aspects of the business: sales, marketing, design, engineering, purchasing, and so on. Lee Iacocca didn't personally build cars—he put together a team of people who knew how to build, market and sell cars—and minivans.

Not too many years ago a neighboring inner-city public school district near where I live hired a retired GM executive to be their superintendent. More than a few people scratched their head or wondered out loud about this decision. I had a different take on the whole thing, but only because of that question my professor had posed to us in class one evening. Now we would see if the old professor really knew what he was talking about. How would this GM executive do moving from the automobile industry into education? What is your guess?

She did great, better than several predecessors I could recall, and she surprised many of the skeptics. To the best of my knowledge, the new superintendent never taught any children before or after taking on this job. Yet she had success beyond what others before her had, in spite of their academic credentials.

I am not suggesting that we should go out of our way to hire non-educators to supervise educational endeavors. That is not the point—and it probably is not a common practice to hire business executives to manage schools, although it does happen on occasion.

The point is that good leaders can often apply their leadership skills to various situations, and good leaders usually recognize that they cannot do everything. Time won't allow a leader to tend to every task, and the leader's own personal limitations make it impossible for him or her to master every necessary skill. This king will, as best as he is able, surround himself with good people. He will not try to do everything himself, and he will take great care to appoint the best people he can find to assist him in his court.

God doesn't have limitations, personal or otherwise. The Creator of the universe doesn't sleep or have need of sleep. He is everywhere at all times, knows all things, has infinite power, and isn't constrained by time as we are. God doesn't need to surround Himself with workers, good or otherwise.

And yet, He does. God invites us to share in His ministry work to those around us. God calls us by the Spirit to be faithful parents, community leaders, laborers, Sunday School teachers, shop foremen, Bible class leaders, CEOs, church elders, and so on to work in His Church and His world. You and I are called by God to serve others faithfully.

Has God positioned you where you can surround yourself with good workers who assist you faithfully in doing God-pleasing work? Then approach that task prayerfully, choosing those people who will work as teammates with you to operate this endeavor. Has God positioned you where you can faithfully serve under another's direction? In that case, work humbly, supporting those in authority over you, and with a servant's heart, joyfully fulfill your duties. Certainly God calls each of us to serve as a good example and provide faithful leadership in our family, in church, and within the community.

Pray for God's guidance and blessings, remembering the disciples whom Jesus called to serve Him and the rest of His flock. Observe how each of these disciples, though not perfect, faithfully followed the Master and used their various talents and abilities for the building up of His kingdom. The "way that is blameless" has already been prepared for us through the death and resurrection of God's Son.

....

Has God positioned you where you can surround yourself with good workers who assist you faithfully in doing God-pleasing work? Then approach that task prayerfully.

Prayer: Lord Jesus Christ, You have given me vocations where I can serve You in faith and my neighbor in love. Help me to walk in Your blameless way so that I might encourage my fellow man for whom You also gave Your life. In Your name I pray. Amen.

....

Thursday

DAILY STUDY QUESTIONS
Psalm 101:6

1. What was the best team experience in which you were privileged to play a part?

2. What made that team experience so memorable and so enjoyable?

3. Describe the kind of people you think David was looking for when he wanted only the faithful and the blameless?

4. Why is it so important to surround yourself with people who are intent on living rightly and righteously?

5. Are there any personal or working relationships in your life that need to be reexamined in the light of David's direction?

Psalm 101:7-8

No one who practices deceit shall dwell in my house; no one who utters lies shall continue before my eyes. Morning by morning I will destroy all the wicked in the land, cutting off all the evildoers from the city of the LORD.

Morning by Morning

Double-dealing, gossip, slander, double-talk, lying—call it what you will, but the king is not going to tolerate deceit. "Morning by morning," he is going to address this issue, putting to silence all the wicked. It may have been tradition for kings to hear cases in the morning, so perhaps this is what he means with his reference to the morning. In any case, it is obvious that this is a daily problem.

The king begins by condemning deceit, and this is not just the telling of lies. It also includes, as we say in our oath in court, "telling the truth, the whole truth, and nothing but the truth." We should not lie about our neighbor and we should not omit any of the truth that might be helpful to him. However, even in telling the truth, we should take care not to harm our neighbor or his reputation. We are to speak well of others, not slander, and always interpret our neighbor's actions in the kindest way. Words are powerful, and our words can help or harm others.

My wife and I really enjoyed bowling in church leagues years ago but haven't had that opportunity in a while. Diane is a pretty good bowler and usually, by the end of a season, is carrying a higher average than I am.

Wilfred, "Wif," is one of my favorite people from my years in ministry; a great church leader and mentor, he also could be mischievous. One Sunday evening our teams were bowling against each other, and Diane was having a great night. Her first game was terrific, and the second one was starting out even better . . . until about the fourth frame. As she leaned over to pick up her bowling ball in that frame, Wif, who was sitting next to me at the scorer's table, asked, "Chuck, did you ever notice what Diane does with her right hand when she releases the ball?" Of course, he said this just loud enough for Diane to hear him.

Diane looked toward us and asked, "What?" By the way, Diane is a lefty, bowling left-handed, too, so her right hand really doesn't have very much to do with anything. Just let it swing and follow through naturally—she probably never gave it too much thought until . . .

Wif was a wonderful person, highly respected and loved by many. He was a veteran, a successful businessman in the community, served for years as president of the local school board, and was the chairman of our congregation. I mentioned that he could also be mischievous, didn't I? In his most innocent voice, he reassured Diane that this "thing" she was supposedly doing with her right hand was "probably nothing." "I just never saw anyone do that before . . . but don't worry about it."

Wif and I both knew where Diane's next ball was going—directly into the left-side gutter. Her second ball went cross alley and into the right-side gutter. A zero in frame number four. Diane sat down next to me after that frame and immediately asked, "What am I doing wrong with my right hand?" Nothing I said could get her back on track; the damage had been done. Wif was also a farmer, and the seed had been planted.

Like I said, Wif was a wonderful guy, and what he did was done in fun, although I know that many serious bowlers may not see it that way. Serious golfers either! Yes, I confess that I've used this ploy once or twice on the golf course. We had lots of laughs about what he did, and although he tried, it never worked again when we bowled against him in the future.

On a more serious note, this story points out how powerful, even damaging, just a few words can be. The king is going to set out every morning to guard people in his court from damaging words: deceitful words, lies, slander, false testimony, gossip, half-truths, and even the truth spoken in a harmful manner.

I mentioned earlier that Wif was also a mentor. Sitting on a wooden swing in his side yard and overlooking his dairy farm, he taught me some lessons about words and the harm they can cause. As chairman of the congregation and president of the local public school board, Wif had heard many words. He also had been responsible for speaking many words on behalf of a congregation and a school district, so he took words seriously.

"Morning by morning." Harmful, hurtful words will always be around us; otherwise the king would not have to be addressing this issue every morning.

Through God's grace and mercy, the king pledges in Psalm 101 to guard his own heart, his eyes, and his walk, seeking to lead a blameless life. God calls us to do the same, but we can only accomplish this Christian walk by the power of the Holy Spirit and the forgiveness that is ours through Jesus Christ.

The king also pledges to protect those in his courts from evildoers. He will not associate with faithless men of perverse heart, he will silence the haughty and the proud, he is going to seek out faithful people to serve in his courts, and he will not tolerate deceit. That's a lofty goal for us and even for a king with all of his power and might.

But what is not attainable for us in our sinfulness is certainly possible with God, for with God all things are possible. God is our King and protector who uses the weak and lowly of this world to do His will, even you and me. He calls us through His Son, Jesus, to walk in love before Him as well as in our dealings with our neighbors, co-workers, and family.

Growing in Christ, as St. Paul puts it, God prepares us for "the work of ministry, for building up the body of Christ, until we all attain to the unity of the faith and of the knowledge of the Son of God, to mature manhood, to the measure of the stature of the fullness of Christ" (Ephesians 4:12–13).

We pray and trust that God, our King, will guard and protect us in this sinful world and that He will also guard our steps to keep us from sinning. When we fall down, He will lift us up, and when we sin, He will forgive us "morning by morning" for Jesus' sake, washing us in the blood of the Lamb and declaring us blameless in His sight.

....

[God] calls us through His Son, Jesus, to walk in love before Him as well as in our dealings with our neighbors, co-workers, and family.

Prayer: Blessed Holy Spirit, Your grace and compassion are new every morning. Through Your Word and Sacraments, help me to keep on my Lord's blameless path, and graciously forgive me when I stray. In Jesus' name. Amen.

....

Friday

DAILY STUDY QUESTIONS
Psalm 101:7-8

1. When was a time you witnessed the power of words to do great harm?

2. How would you define *falsehood*?

3. How careful are you always to tell the truth, that is, how often would a strict definition of *falsehood* challenge or condemn your words?

4. What is the difference between deceitfully withholding the truth and choosing not to divulge some known fact for the sake of another person's reputation or well-being?

5. David made a commitment to make the pursuit of righteousness and the eradication of evil a daily routine. What will it mean for you, today, to stand for truth and to tolerate no evil?

Week Three

....

PSALM 101

....

The 101st psalm is a psalm of instruction in
which David uses himself as an example of how
to have godly helpers and not tolerate evil
servants. He accordingly lists the various lusts
and vices of an evil worker, which belongs in
a longer commentary to explain. This he calls
singing of "steadfast love and justice," that is,
singing of how God is gracious to the godly
and punishes the wicked, and how every work
should be doing good and shunning evil. How
it shall go with them on these accounts is well
depicted in Absalom, Ahithophel, Joab, and
others. For whoever wants to make and keep
the people godly shall be burdened with all
hatred and envy. Therefore, he may well sing
to God and give thanks to Him who has given
grace and justice. Where God does this, such
a song would remain unsung. In its place only
cursing and scolding would remain in the house
and the only hope be hanging and beheadings
and the like.

—Martin Luther

GROUP BIBLE STUDY
(Questions and answers on pp. 186–88.)

1. Imagine that someone does die and makes you king. What would be the best part about being a king? What would be the worst part?

2. Read the entire psalm. What sort of attitude does David convey with regard to his position as king?

3. Music was a critical part of the worship life of the Old Testament people of God (v. 1). What do you think is the style of music that is most conducive to praising God? If you were to compose a song of praise to God, what style would you choose?

4. Consider carefully the action plan presented by David in verses 2–4. As a group, recount each of the righteous practices suggested by David, and then discuss: which is most important, which is most difficult, which is most overlooked or neglected?

5. A better understanding of what it means to live righteously as God's man can produce many responses. Share with the group how you react when you think seriously about what God expects of you. What dangers need to be avoided when thinking about holy practices that should characterize the Christian man's life?

6. Too often what we condemn in others we will excuse in ourselves. How is this particularly true of the twin sins mentioned in verse 5? How do people make excuses for what is nothing more than slander and arrogant pride? Why do we so quickly excuse these sins when they appear in our own lives?

7. David appears to set a very high bar for those who will be his personal associates. Is this a matter of personal choice, or is this God's counsel to us? How does one follow this direction while also following the mandate to extend to everyone love and mercy and to strive to bring the Gospel love of Christ to every person?

8. David indicates a "zero tolerance" policy when it comes to deceit and falsehood. How does God's standard for truthful speaking differ from the world's standards for our speaking to one another? What would happen if you consistently practiced (and expected others to practice) God's standard of truth in every relationship?

9. While this psalm is filled with wonderful insights for Christian living and with practical advice for the man of God, it is generally considered a messianic psalm. What makes it messianic? Why is (or isn't) it surprising to find such practical material in a messianic psalm?

10. Considering the standard expressed in the psalm, would you have found a place in David's court? Knowing that grace does not release us from our responsibility to live holy and upright lives, which of the practices enumerated in the psalm most needs your attention in the coming week?

Week Four

Psalm 110

[1] The Lᴏʀᴅ says to my Lord:
"Sit at My right hand,
until I make Your enemies Your footstool."

[2] The Lᴏʀᴅ sends forth from Zion
Your mighty scepter.
Rule in the midst of Your enemies!

[3] Your people will offer themselves freely
on the day of Your power,
in holy garments;
from the womb of the morning,
the dew of Your youth will be Yours.

[4] The Lᴏʀᴅ has sworn
and will not change His mind,
"You are a priest forever
after the order of Melchizedek."

[5] The Lord is at Your right hand;
He will shatter kings on the day of His wrath.

[6] He will execute judgment among the nations,
filling them with corpses;
He will shatter chiefs
over the wide earth.

[7] He will drink from the brook by the way;
therefore He will lift up His head.

Joshua Salzberg

Psalm 110:1

The LORD says to my Lord: "Sit at My right hand, until I make your enemies your footstool."

The Bus-Stop Prophet

RUUURRRRRR . . . Splash!

Those are two sounds that, despite my best efforts, have yet to escape from memory. The first was the sound of a Chicago Transit bus approaching. The latter was the bus *not* stopping to pick me up, but cruising through a puddle, sloshing my jeans with muddy street water—at least I *hoped* it was muddy street water.

Either way, this was a fitting ending to what had been an overwhelming and unusually cold spring day. I was twenty-one, about to finish another semester of film school, and spring had brought back the same questions I remember facing my senior year of high school: What have I been doing with my life? What am I going to do with my life? And most important, when and how do I get out of here?

That last question was in the forefront of my mind as I, with increasing frustration, attempted to dry off my pant legs with a newspaper. My college offered a special study semester in L.A. for film students, a program that attracted me to Columbia College in the first place. But as I looked down the street, hoping to see my bus, I was sure that I'd never complete the extensive application process in time.

The application required, among other things, a five-page essay, three letters of recommendation, and because it was only my second year at the school, a DVD of my film work to prove that I was up to par. My two years of experience couldn't compare to that of the other applicants, most of whom were in their fourth year. I was daunted by the application requirements themselves, not to mention the deadline—only one week away.

Growing more and more annoyed with my muddy pants, I couldn't fight the feeling that the entire city was working against me, holding me prisoner.

Every man feels like the world is against him at some point. I don't care how legitimate the predicament appears to onlookers—that feeling of hopelessness is very real. King David knew this feeling well and for good reason. As the king of Israel, David made many enemies and was quite literally attacked by the armies of the world. He wasn't just dealing with thwarted plans, but the thousands upon thousands of people who wanted him dead. Throughout David's entire reign, Israel was constantly in danger of being overtaken by one of its many enemies. It wouldn't have taken more than one legion of soldiers for me to consider trading Israel for a piece of midlevel stock in the newly merged Israeli-Enemy conglomerate.

It's no wonder David often laments about deliverance from enemies. In Psalm 110, David writes: "The Lord says to my Lord: 'Sit at My right hand, until I make Your enemies Your footstool.'"

This enemies-as-a-footstool imagery must have been appealing to the king with many foes, but David wasn't writing about his own adversaries. He knew that God had already appointed a greater King, one who would be hated not just by the kings and kingdoms of his day, but by kingdoms to come. Talk about feeling like the world is against you: Jesus faced opposition from the Roman government, religious leaders, even his own friends. He knew what it felt like to have the world working against Him because the sin of the world *was* working against him.

Sssss . . . Cahhhhh.

The doors of the bus—my bus—swung open, waking me from my California dreamin'. After stepping onto the crowded bus and paying my fare, I sat in the only unoccupied seat. And before there was even a chance to get back to wallowing in my self-pity, a voice called . . .

"Where are you from?"

Behind me sat a middle-aged man, unshaven, but otherwise unspecific. He continued, "You're not from here, are you?"

The man's question threw me off guard, until I noticed the bracelet around his wrist. It wasn't a friendship bracelet or a hospital bracelet, and definitely not a WWJD bracelet. It was a prison bracelet. My shock only allowed me to mutter the name of my hometown, but this wasn't the answer he was looking for.

"No, no, no. Where's your homeland?"

Now I understood where he was going with this. My dad's family is Jewish, and I look the part, mostly due to my black curly hair. The man didn't look surprised to hear about my ancestral history and continued his interrogation: "Are you in business school?"

Thinking he was purporting some pretty broad stereotypes, I let him know that I was a film student.

"Ahhh," he sighed. "Well, there you go. You're gonna make it. You're one of those chosen people."

As he finished his public anointment, the bus slid to a stop—and not a second too soon. I offered an awkward good-bye and stepped off the bus undeniably weirded out, but also unable to shake his encouraging (albeit slightly racist) words.

Now, don't get me wrong. I by no means thought my Semitic ancestry entitled me to a successful career in Hollywood, but that recently incarcerated bus-stop prophet had inadvertently reminded me of my spiritual ancestry.

And years later, the warmth that followed my encounter with the bus-stop prophet comes flooding back upon hearing David's words of hope: "until I make Your enemies Your footstool."

David didn't mistake God's covenant as a promise to wipe the battlefield clean and rid Israel's king of all his worries. Nor is this psalm a pledge to take out the co-worker standing in the way of a promotion or even the illness that plagues a loved one. And it's certainly not a promise to get rid of the obstacles that, for me, stood between Chicago and Los Angeles.

God's words are a promise to defeat the enemies of the One who delivers us from our own worry. Hebrews 10:12–14 reveals that David's psalm was fulfilled in God's Son: "But when Christ had offered for all time a single sacrifice for sins, He sat down at the right hand of God, waiting from that time until His enemies should be made a footstool for His feet. For by a single offering He has perfected for all time those who are being sanctified."

When Christ defeated His enemies by suffering and dying on a cross, He defeated my enemies as well: sin, Satan, and death. I am made perfect through Christ's sacrifice. Though my near future is uncertain, my eternal future is unwavering and unconditionally guaranteed. And so, the same promise of which King David sang, that same promise made complete in Christ Jesus, is passed on to you and me:

No matter how attacked you feel, no matter how much the world seems to be working against you, no matter what—you are an heir of God's eternal kingdom by His Son's death and resurrection.

You're gonna make it. You're one of those chosen people.

....

When Christ defeated His enemies by suffering and dying on a cross, He defeated my enemies as well: sin, Satan, and death.

Prayer: Lord Jesus Christ, You rule and reign from our Father's throne in heaven. Bless and protect Your Church, of which You have made me a member, so that Your name may be glorified as the world's Savior. I ask this in Your name. Amen.

....

DAILY STUDY QUESTIONS
Psalm 110:1

1. What "enemies" (even buses and whole cities sometimes qualify) have been making your life difficult?

2. Since Jesus taught us to love everyone, is it right for Christians to have enemies?

3. This psalm loses all of its wonder if it is not clear who is speaking at any given moment. Who is saying what in today's verse?

4. The promise to have a footstool stuffed with enemies is made by God to the Savior. In what sense can Christians take comfort in this promise made to the Messiah?

5. If you are "one of those chosen people" (and by Baptism, you are—Galatians 3:29), then what difference should it make for your living, today?

Psalm 110:2

> The LORD sends forth from Zion Your mighty scepter. Rule in the midst of Your enemies!

Homesick

I made it to L.A.

As it turned out, getting there was the easy part. In my excitement over my acceptance into the film production class at CBS Studios, I hadn't even considered how expensive it would be to live in Los Angeles for six weeks. Needless to say, renting an apartment in California is considerably more expensive than in the Midwest. Heck, buying an Angeleno cup of coffee is likely to break the bank.

Fortunately for me (and my pocketbook), First Lutheran Church opened its mission house to me, rent-free. I had shelter and just enough money to buy six weeks' worth of pasta. So, what was I doing my first day in the entertainment capital of the world?

Looking at homeless people.

The homeless people of Venice Beach, to be more specific. Venice Beach is a must-see for many who come from all over the world to see throngs of bare-chested musclemen, skateboarding slacker-kids, drum-circle hippies, palm-reading gypsies, backflipping street dancers, and those ever-popular anarchy-themed bumper sticker stands. But, speckled throughout these tourist hot spots walks a less alluring, yet equally prevalent, Venice mainstay: the panhandling homeless.

My eyes were drawn to these unmentioned members of the Venice culture not out of pity or disgust, but out of empathy.

I related to the nagging sense of uncertainty, the ever-present state of unknown that defines the life of a drifter. I wasn't sleeping on the beach, but I wasn't going home either. Graduation awaited at the other end of summer and, sure, I'd always be able to go back to my family—I'd always be able to call that home.

But I wouldn't be living at home anymore. I'd be on my own.

I wonder if the disciples felt a similar sense of loneliness at their last Passover meal with Jesus. This motley crew had left their jobs and families and dedicated their lives to the service and teachings of a man who promised freedom to the Jews. Then, out of nowhere, at the Passover meal no less, Jesus revealed He was about to leave their company. Every one of these men must have felt oppressed by the impending uncertainty suddenly thrust into their lives. Jesus' followers were without a leader. They were instantly orphans.

Perhaps it was out of this orphan feeling that Philip turned to his Rabbi. "Lord, show us the Father, and it is enough for us" (John 14:8). Do what You want, Lord, but let us know what we've been saying isn't a lie. Prove that God exists.

Jesus must have sighed before replying. They still didn't get it.

"Have I been with you so long, and you still do not know Me, Philip? Whoever has seen Me has seen the Father" (John 14:9).

This is a heck of a revelation. And yet, it's a revelation that Jesus' forefather, King David, understood hundreds of years before. The second verse of Psalm 110 is a record of David's foresight: "The Lord sends forth from Zion Your mighty scepter. Rule in the midst of Your enemies."

Zion was the name given to the sacred hill where the temple rested, and the Jews believed that God dwelled in this temple—that it was His home. So, when David sang of the Messiah's scepter being sent forth from Zion, he was declaring the unborn Redeemer to be God Himself—God in the flesh.

If there's anyone who knows what it's like to feel estranged, to feel a million miles from home, it's the Creator Incarnate away from His heavenly home, inhabiting humanity in a strange, scary, messed-up world.

And yet, Jesus loved this broken world. He comforted the unloved. He extended His "mighty scepter" from Zion, bringing a piece of His heavenly home to earth. When He left the earth, did heaven go with Him?

I don't know much about heaven, but I do know that Jesus left Philip with a promise: "Truly, truly, I say to you, whoever believes in Me will also do the works that I do; and greater works than these will he do, because I am going to the Father" (John 14:12).

Greater things than what Jesus did? He didn't heal the blind, but one night, the same man who served as pastor, liturgist, and organist took me grocery shopping. They never raised the dead, but the quilting club left me home-cooked meals. Every

Sunday morning, all thirty members of my new surrogate family were in church, waiting with big hugs and bigger smiles.

It wasn't water into wine, but I felt loved. I felt—if just a little—like I was home.

The world's full of homeless people.

What if, like First Lutheran, we're here to give a home to the homeless—or, like Jesus, to bring a piece of heaven to earth? I can't heal the sick, but I know plenty of people who are sick of hurting. My life is filled with plenty of people to love—plenty who need the same glimpse of heaven a small Lutheran church showed me.

I realize I'm not a miracle worker. I'm not a king like the one Psalm 110 describes, but I am a servant of the King through my Baptism, my adoption into an eternal home. And that same King who brought His kingdom to earth continues to extend His holy scepter from Zion through us, displaying His love of humanity.

Don't get me wrong: I know I'm gonna mess it up. I do every day.

I overlook someone in need. I hurt instead of help. Some days, no matter how hard I try to be positive, I still feel homeless. But we have a comfort that the disciples didn't fully comprehend in the Upper Room. We know that in the hours that followed, Jesus stumbled to the cross, not out of obligation to the religious leaders who wanted him dead nor the Roman officials who granted their request, but out of love and compassion for the orphans of the world.

By His resurrection, and through the gifts of His Word and Spirit, God makes His home with us. Wherever we are, however homeless we may feel, God is with us.

And if that's true, home is never too far away.

. . . .

And that same King who brought His kingdom to earth continues to extend His holy scepter from Zion through us, displaying His love of humanity.

Prayer: Lord Jesus Christ, when You ascended into heaven, You gave Your gifts to men. Enable me through Your Gospel to be both the salt and light You have called me to purify and illuminate the world. I ask this in Your name. Amen.

. . . .

Tuesday

DAILY STUDY QUESTIONS
Psalm 110:2

1. Recall a time when you felt "homeless," that is, alone, powerless, and without an advocate. Did this time of life strengthen or rattle your faith in God?

2. Check the actors again in verse 2. Who is speaking, and what is he saying to whom?

3. What further evidence does this verse offer for the close relationship between the Lord, Yahweh, and David's Lord, the Messiah?

4. What is the nature of the strength of the Messiah's scepter? In other words, in what ways is Christ's strength made manifest?

5. As one who follows the Messiah and extends His kingdom into the world, what can you do, today, that will make Christ's scepter of power evident to those you meet?

Psalm 110:3

> Your people will offer themselves freely on the day of Your power, in holy garments; from the womb of the morning, the dew of Your youth will be Yours.

The Crusade for Christ

I can't even count the number of times I've run out of gas. It's embarrassing.

One time, my car stalled in the middle of an intersection and would have stayed stalled if two generous guys hadn't pushed my hand-me-down Oldsmobile to a nearby service station. Another time, I was stranded in an unfamiliar neighborhood when a police officer picked me up and spent his lunch break finding, buying, and filling up a gas can for me.

There have been several similar scenarios, but no matter how hard I try, I can't forget running on empty in Utah.

My adventure through Utah came after the semester in L.A. After hearing about my Hollywood stories, my college roommate decided to make the move with me. So, here we were: two college grads driving through Utah on empty—not a gas station in sight.

Up until this point in our cross-country road trip, our conversation revolved around the previous year of life in Chicago. We'd served as leaders for a Christian ministry on campus, and neither of us felt we'd done much good. Attendance at our Bible study oscillated. The weekly gatherings which we'd spent time and money organizing didn't live up to our expectations. We couldn't help but consider the possibility that we'd done more damage than good to Christ's cause.

In short, we felt like lame leaders.

Conversely, David describes Jesus as a great leader in the third verse of Psalm 110. "Your people will offer themselves freely on the day of Your power."

Perhaps the military implications are lost on those of us who don't own a Medal of Honor or the *Band of Brothers* box set, but David knew the benefit of willing troops. As a general and king, David led thousands and thousands to battle—and those willing soldiers would lay down their lives to defend their kingdom and king.

This attitude is noble, no doubt, but it says more about the one leading the troops than the character of the soldiers themselves. Again, the psalm says they will "offer themselves freely"—not forced into battle, but glad to serve their leader at all costs.

I can't imagine anyone in my college Bible study willing to serve me at all costs.

What characteristic creates willing troops? My roommate and I were trying to look ahead—for a gas station as well as an answer to that question.

How could we be better leaders in L.A.? How could we, as we journeyed out into the world, fix what we didn't get right before?

The first Christians faced this same question as they journeyed out into the world. Peter, in his First Epistle, offers his thoughts to the leaders of the Church scattered throughout the world. Keep in mind this is Peter talking. The same guy who walked on water. The same guy who cut off a soldier's ear to defend Jesus. So, what was bold, brave Peter's advice to these valiant soldiers of God? "Be subject" (2:13).

Excuse me? What does Peter mean, "Be subject"?

Peter isn't offering some holistic, humanist morality catchphrase in order to sell the much-anticipated follow-up to his First Letter. He's endorsing a whole new attitude; a whole new approach to what it means to be religious. Up until this point, the religious leaders had led as lords over the people. They applied a be-holy-as-we-are-holy approach to leading. When Peter tells the leaders of the new Church to be subject to authorities, for even slaves to be subject to their masters no matter how unjust—he's not just preaching good manners, he's establishing a whole new precedent.

Peter wasn't the first to teach humility. He points to another Church leader in the second chapter of his book: "He committed no sin, neither was deceit found in His mouth. When He was reviled, He did not revile in return; when He suffered, He did not threaten, but continued entrusting Himself to Him who judges justly. He Himself bore our sins in His body on the tree, that we might die to sin and live to righteousness. By His wounds you have been healed" (vv. 22–24).

A blameless man taking the blame for others? *This* is a leader.

Jesus made Himself subject; God Himself succumbed to insult, even though one word could have silenced those who insulted. Jesus didn't overcome sin and death by overthrowing the rulers of the day. He didn't secure salvation for humanity by forcing others to bow to His will. He could have—and would have been justified in doing so. He's God. But our leader chose to be humbled, to be lame.

And this is a leader.

In our Western civilization, the battle we fight on a day-to-day basis isn't won by battle cries and macho bravado, at least not for the most part. As leaders of the same Church that Peter was advising two thousand years ago, our battles are fought with servant-minded submission.

Easier said than done, right? I bet even David struggled with humility. He was the leader of Israel, God's chosen people, for crying out loud! Either way, it's clear that David recognized his promised offspring, the Son of God, as a King *of* kings—the King whom even kings follow.

Because even the best leaders need a leader.

Similarly, there was no way we would have made it to California if it weren't for the oasis, Utah's "lone" gas station that appeared not a moment too late.

Because even the best cars need fuel.

I've been rescued from my own missteps as a Christian even more times than a stranger's helped me with an empty tank. We all move forward as leaders, as people, as willing troops only by the holy will of our leader—our lame leader who leads by His example of perfect humility.

I didn't see it at the time, but now, as I reflect on that trouble-laden drive across Utah, I recognize what a great lesson in humility it had been—a good lesson to learn upon entering the entertainment industry . . . and the crusade for Christ.

We all move forward as leaders, as people, as willing troops only by the holy will of our leader—our lame leader who leads by His example of perfect humility.

Prayer: Holy God, by Your Spirit You have led me out of darkness into Your marvelous light. Forgiven by Your grace and according to Your will, lead me on the path where I might also positively influence my family and friends. In Jesus' name. Amen.

Wednesday

DAILY STUDY QUESTIONS
Psalm 110:3

1. Who is in authority over you; that is, to whom are you required to be subject on a regular basis?

2. Is being in submission an inherently bad or distasteful thing? What sometimes makes it so difficult to accept?

3. What is it that makes some leaders easier, or even exciting, to follow? What does the response of the people (v. 3) to the Messiah's leadership say about the Messiah?

4. What does it mean for you that you are a soldier in God's holy army?

5. What part of God's purposes for you would benefit from a little more "soldierly attention" from you?

Psalm 110:4

The LORD has sworn and will not change His mind, "You are a priest forever after the order of Melchizedek."

Nothing Lasts Forever

It's here somewhere, I know it.

This always happens when my mom cleans my room. She cleans up, I lose stuff, and all I can do is look. I look in my dresser. I look in the closet. I look under my . . .

Under my bed!

I check, and sure enough, there it is: the green balloon from the Fourth of July parade. Other kids were less irresponsible, allowing their balloons to pop or float off into the firework-filled sky. Not I. From the moment a parade participant walked to me and entrusted me with the balloon, I had dedicated all my efforts to its protection.

But now, as I pull on the string and retrieve my long-lost possession from under the bed, instead of holding the balloon down to the ground to prevent it from escaping, I'm holding it up. My once beautiful green balloon dangles, against my will, close to the ground, wrinkled and devoid of its gravity-defying magic.

I run into my parents' bedroom and find my father putting on socks. Let me repeat: *putting on socks* as if a life-altering tragedy has not just occurred under his roof!

"Fix it!" I plead, cradling the balloon like a baby. "Make it work."

My dad carefully takes my prized possession from me and examines it, turning it over in his hands before speaking.

"There's nothing we can do," he admits, pointing to a tear in the balloon's smooth green surface.

The weight of the unthinkable smacks me like a ton of bricks. The object of my affection was gone—inevitably separated from me forever. My eyes begin to water as a revelation washes over me. So, I choke back the tears and confess, "Life is short, isn't it?"

Looking back, it amazes me to think my first philosophical ponderings over death came at age eight over the loss of helium. This, of course, was only the first of many losses. Over the next few years, as relatives died, friends' parents divorced, or people broke promises, my eight-year-old instincts were reinforced again and again:

Nothing lasts forever.

It's this fact of life that Jesus faces on a dark, foreboding afternoon. Life is short. Thirty-three years short, for the Son of God hangs on a tree, beaten and bruised and broken and minutes away from death. Under the weight of the cross, His lungs barely strong enough to breathe, Jesus speaks.

"Father, forgive them, for they know not what they do."

Jesus asks God to forgive those killing Him. Though His mercy is noble, there's another radical thing happening here. Ever since Aaron, Moses' brother, there had been a Jewish priesthood, a line of men who, according to their ancestry, were to be mediators between the people of Israel and their God. Priests would offer sacrifices for the people, and these same priests passed on God's forgiveness to Israel. By petitioning God's forgiveness, Jesus claims to possess the authority of a priest.

Wait a second. Psalm 110's first three verses make it clear that God gave Jesus the title of King, and kings can't be priests. In fact, the Jewish tradition had a strict separation of church and state: kings do their thing; priests do God's things. So which one is Jesus? King or Priest?

There is one, just one other person that the Bible references as both king and priest. His name was Melchizedek.

Scripture tells us very little about this man. Truth be told, there are only two verses dedicated to him in the entire Old Testament. In Genesis 4:18–20, Melchizedek, the king of Salem, blesses Abram, the soon-to-be father of Israel. He is a king performing priestly duties before the Jewish priesthood—before the Jewish people are even conceived.

He's a priest of God outside of the Jewish religion.

Low and behold, God's promise to the Messiah references Melchizedek, the king-priest. David records this promise in Psalm 110, "The LORD has sworn and will not change His mind, 'You are a priest forever in the order of Melchizedek.'"

God proclaims that Jesus, the King of the Jews, is a priest—not of the Jewish heritage, but of Melchizedek's order. Jesus is a priest outside of religion. He's the new mediator, the only mediator between God and man. And this Savior, unlike the priesthood of the Jews, is one that extends before every moment that has ever been to beyond every moment that will be.

No matter how many times I say the word *eternal* in church, I can't fully digest that word. Although I talk about God and heaven and everlasting life, how can I really believe that eternity exists when life seems to prove otherwise?

People die. Relationships end. Nothing lasts forever. Those are the facts of life, and no matter how I justify pain, deep down, I don't know why it exists. All I know is that ever since sin first entered the picture, forever has become more and more a distant memory, and death has held sway.

The writer of Hebrews addresses the reality of death and the problem it causes for every person and (almost) every priest. Now there have been many of those priests, since death prevented them from continuing in office; but because Jesus lives forever, He has a permanent priesthood. Therefore, He is able to save completely those who come to God through Him, because He always lives to intercede for them (Hebrews 7:23–25).

Two thousand years ago, Jesus performed the last sacrifice any priest would ever have to make: Himself. God heard His plea for forgiveness from the altar of the cross. By Christ's death, God forgave and continues to forgive humanity.

God cares for the world as I cared for my green balloon; the difference being that He has the power to save. No tear or leak—not even death itself is beyond repair, because Jesus, who couldn't be contained in a grave, always lives to intercede.

Let's not ignore the facts of life. The world is tough, and death still stings.

But by the holy priest of heaven, by God's New Testament Melchizedek, we have a hope. And despite the world's evidence to the contrary, that hope is eternal.

God cares for the world as I cared for my green balloon; the difference being that He has the power to save.

Prayer: Dear Holy Spirit, You washed me with water and the Word in my Baptism and made me God's royal priest. For the sake of Jesus, my Savior, accept the willing sacrifice of my body and soul for His sake. I ask in His name. Amen.

Thursday

DAILY STUDY QUESTIONS
Psalm 110:4

1. What are some of the recent realities in your life that seem to contradict the idea of "forever"?

2. The Latin word for priest (*pontifex*) actually derives from two words meaning "bridge builder." How is this image an apt picture of the work of a priest?

3. In verse 1, Yahweh spoke the promise of kingly sovereignty to His Christ. Here, in verse 4, the Lord confirms the Messiah's eternal office as Priest with an oath. What does this tell us about the way we should understand the work of the Messiah?

4. Take at look at the cameo appearance of Melchizedek in Genesis 14:18–20. What are some of the special things that strike you about this figure?

5. What comfort is there for you in having an eternal Savior who is King and Priest by God's direction?

Psalm 110:5-7

> The Lord is at Your right hand; He will shatter kings on the day of His wrath. He will execute judgment among the nations, filling them with corpses; He will shatter chiefs over the wide earth. He will drink from the brook by the way; therefore He will lift up His head.

A Fighting Chance

Guess what . . .

High school teachers know that students drink.

This may not seem like a huge revelation to most, but to me—seventeen-year-old me—it was the craziest thing I'd learned at school since prepositional phrases.

First of all, teachers at my Lutheran high school weren't supposed to be hip to teenage trends. In my mind, teachers were supposed to be listening to symphony music and watching TV Land reruns, not keeping up with the vices of adolescents. But, the more I dealt with the faculty, the more I knew what they knew. They knew kids were smoking pot, having sex, dealing drugs . . . in short, they knew much more than I ever imagined.

And that made me angry.

I'll be honest: I led a fairly boring teenage life. No drugs. No drinking. No sex. I stayed out of trouble. But the popular kids, the cool kids, the bad kids had managed to stay out of trouble too. As far as I could tell, they were breaking all the rules and paying none of the consequences.

So, when I find out that my teachers knew about their debauchery, I was furious. I wanted every one of those students brought to justice. I wanted them punished. I wanted the kind of judgment David talks about in Psalm 110: "The Lord is at Your right hand; He will shatter kings on the day of His wrath. He will execute judgment among the nations, filling them with corpses; He will shatter chiefs over the wide earth."

David's speaking some pretty poignant prophecies here. Already, he's talked about God's Son defeating enemies, leading armies, coming down from heaven, and living forever. Now, in the last verses of the psalm, David says that this King-Priest will judge the world, humble its rulers, and bring justice to the earth.

The end of it all doesn't sound so bad. Within this century, one man led a nation on a crusade to rid the earth of the Jewish people in a wave of horrific torture and death. If Jesus is coming as David writes, why doesn't He come? Why didn't He come before this horrible man committed these horrific acts against humanity?

Where is the judge of nations? Where is the wrath? We're ready!

We're ready for evildoers to get what is coming to them the same way I was ready for my teachers to bring judgment on my troublemaking classmates in high school.

At some point during my senior year, I decided to disclose my displeasure with the faculty's lack of judgment to one of my teachers. I was passionate about the subject, very animated, and might have even raised my voice to him. In my defense, these kids were breaking the rules, and I wanted to know why they weren't being convicted and expelled from the school.

He let me finish my rant and then took a breath, carefully choosing his words. I've forgotten most of the algebra equations I learned, I can't remember how to diagram a sentence, and after three years of Spanish, it'd be a miracle if I could talk my way out of a Taco Bell. That said, I still haven't forgotten—will *never* forget—that teacher's response to my rage.

He said, "We could kick them out of school, but that wouldn't solve the problem."

I'm not trying to give advice on how to run a high school or deal with teenage decadence, and I'm sure there are plenty of situations where an expulsion is completely legitimate. None of that negates the message that teacher delivered directly to me. His one statement made everything suddenly, irreversibly clear.

My teacher believed that those students weren't without hope for change. He possessed the patience to give his students a fighting chance.

God possesses this patience. God embodies this patience. Although I don't understand why, can't explain how, and often don't want to believe it's true, the pure and simple facts remain. Humanity spits in the face of God. We're self-serving yet self-effacing, co-dependent yet prejudiced, egotistical yet stubborn in our lack of compassion. The human race deserves to be destroyed, deserted, forgotten, and

111

wiped from existence. We all deserve to be on the receiving end of God's wrath.

And yet,

against all logic:

we are here.

Similar to the way my teacher saw something I didn't, God sees something we don't. Where we see persecutors, God sees One persecuted. Where we see murderers, God sees His Son, murdered. Where we see death, God—against all odds—sees life.

In fact, the same Jesus suffered and died, rose, and before leaving this world, passed on His doctrine of hope to those He left behind.

Before Jesus ascended, He told His followers, "All authority in heaven and on earth has been given to Me. Go therefore and make disciples of all nations, baptizing them in the name of the Father and of the Son and of the Holy Spirit, teaching them to observe all that I have commanded you" (Matthew 28:18–20).

Make disciples of *all* nations. Inexplicably, Jesus saw life where the disciples didn't; not that anyone might be made a disciple, but that a disciple can come from anywhere.

I know this to be true, because I am a testament to this miracle. Although it would take years before I could see it, I was uncompassionate in high school. By the redeeming work of Christ and through the wisdom of my teacher, God began a change in me that day. It's a change that He's still working out and will continue to work out until Christ's return.

I don't know why, and I don't know how, but that doesn't mean it's not true.

Yes, we yearn for Christ's return. We long for justice to be served and for evil to receive the judgment it deserves. But in the meantime, Jesus' death and resurrection speaks through us, broken human to broken human, because He didn't just die for the Church. He died that all may know the hope of being whole.

Not *every*one will love, but—as God proved through His Son's humble birth—love can come from *any*one. By the gift of heaven's eternal King-Priest, God gives the world love. He gives humanity hope.

By grace without condition, God gives His creation a fighting chance.

Where we see persecutors, God sees One persecuted. Where we see murderers, God sees His Son, murdered. Where we see death, God—against all odds—sees life.

Prayer: Lord Jesus Christ, Son of God, You crushed sin, Satan, and death under Your feet on the cross and declared Your victory by rising again. Help me to live in righteousness and to deal justly with all the people I meet. In Your name I pray. Amen.

Friday

DAILY STUDY QUESTIONS
Psalm 110:5–7

1. What is the greatest travesty of justice that you have experienced or witnessed?

2. After contemplating the Messiah's priestly credentials, the psalm returns to the original image: the Messiah as divine warrior. Based on the text, what is the nature of the Messiah's justice?

3. While it is tempting to hope that the justice of the Last Day comes soon, the thought of divine justice can also cause one to wish for a long delay in implementation. How do you react to the idea of God's justice?

4. One last time, try to follow the characters at work in these three verses. Who is speaking, who is acting, and who is the "He"?

5. Knowing that God's justice is imminent, and that His mercy is present, whom do you know who needs to hear, today, about the Gospel of God's Messiah?

Week Four

PSALM 110

The 110th psalm is a prophecy of Christ, that He shall be an eternal king and priest, indeed true God, sitting at the right hand of God the Father, and that He would be glorified and recognized. In the entire Scripture there is nothing like this psalm. It would be right to acknowledge it as the chief confirmation of the Christian faith. For nowhere else is Christ prophesied with such clear, plain words as a priest and an eternal priest. It is prophesied as well that the priesthood of Aaron would be abolished. This psalm is yet again and more splendidly extolled in the Epistle to the Hebrews. It is indeed a shame that such a psalm is not more richly extolled by Christians.

—Martin Luther

Week Four, Psalm 110

GROUP BIBLE STUDY
(Questions and answers on pp. 193–95.)

1. Tell the group about the greatest leader you have had the privilege of knowing and following. What made him such a great leader?

2. Having enormous messianic implications and significant teaching regarding Christ, Psalm 110 is one of the most quoted psalms in the New Testament. What makes verse 1 so important? What does it teach about the Messiah?

3. Why do you think the idea of absolute subjection is associated with being made into a footstool?

4. In what sense is it true that the prophecy is being fulfilled even now? Is Christ ruling in the midst of His enemies? What about those enemies who refuse even to acknowledge His existence, let alone His authority?

5. Verse 3 poses some challenges for translation. See how many different attempts are represented by the translations being used by different members of your group. Regardless of the direction of the translation, what is the basic message of this verse? What does this teach us about the Messiah and His role as leader?

6. What is the degree of sacrifice that God expects from His people? (Check out Romans 12:1–2 and Matthew 16:24–25.) How many Christians do you think actually understand and believe this?

7. Hebrews 7 thoroughly explores the Christological significance of Melchizedek. Take a look at the first ten verses of Hebrews 7, and list as many connections as you can find between Melchizedek and Jesus. How does Jesus surpass the person of Melchizedek?

8. In verses 5–7 of the psalm, a peculiar thing happens with the pronoun "He." To whom is the "He" referring in verse 5; what about in verse 7? What does this teach us about God and His work through the Messiah?

9. How do you reconcile this rather gory image of divine justice and messianic activity with the New Testament picture of God delivering grace and mercy through the Messiah?

10. The volunteers of verse 3 have receded into the background by verse 5, and it is God and His Christ who do all of the fighting. What does this mean for you, one of those willing volunteers, as you proceed into the week ahead?

Week Five

Psalm 132

1 Remember, O Lord, in David's favor,
all the hardships he endured,

2 how he swore to the Lord
and vowed to the Mighty One of Jacob,

3 "I will not enter my house
or get into my bed,

4 I will not give sleep to my eyes
or slumber to my eyelids,

5 until I find a place for the Lord,
a dwelling place for the Mighty One of Jacob."

6 Behold, we heard of it in Ephrathah;
we found it in the fields of Jaar.

7 "Let us go to His dwelling place;
let us worship at His footstool!"

8 Arise, O Lord, and go to Your resting place,
You and the ark of Your might.

9 Let Your priests be clothed with righteousness,
and let Your saints shout for joy.

10 For the sake of Your servant David,
do not turn away the face of Your anointed one.

11 The Lord swore to David a sure oath
from which He will not turn back:
"One of the sons of your body
I will set on your throne.

12 If your sons keep My covenant
and My testimonies that I shall teach them,

their sons also forever
shall sit on your throne."

¹³ For the LORD has chosen Zion;
He has desired it for His dwelling place:

¹⁴ "This is My resting place forever;
here I will dwell, for I have desired it.

¹⁵ I will abundantly bless her provisions;
I will satisfy her poor with bread.

¹⁶ Her priests I will clothe with salvation,
and her saints will shout for joy.

¹⁷ There I will make a horn to sprout for David;
I have prepared a lamp for My anointed.

¹⁸ His enemies I will clothe with shame,
but on Him His crown will shine."

Lyle Buettner

Psalm 132:1–5

> Remember, O LORD, in David's favor, all the hardships he endured, how he swore to the LORD and vowed to the Mighty One of Jacob, "I will not enter my house or get into my bed, I will not give sleep to my eyes or slumber to my eyelids, until I find a place for the LORD, a dwelling place for the Mighty One of Jacob."

God's Resurrection Temple

I have three beautiful *living* children. I say *living* because I really have had four. One died in my wife's womb. Her miscarriage greatly affected both of us. It happened during a summer when we were in Seward, Nebraska—I was a student at Concordia University at the time. That summer I stopped going to church. I allowed Satan a foothold into my life. He tempted me, and I succumbed. I despised the preaching of God's Word; I snubbed my nose at the Sacrament. Had I gone to church, God would have comforted me with both.

Family members are comforted by soothing Gospel messages at Christian funerals. Christ is arisen! Because He lives, you, too, shall live! After the funeral service, the body is laid to rest in the ground in hopeful anticipation of the resurrection. This event gives the family a sense of closure. My wife and I didn't have closure in Christian burial. We weren't able to hold our child before *she* died. (My wife and I had discussed only girl names up until that point. We would have named her Catherine.)

Everyone endures the death of loved ones. Some, like me, even endure the death of their children. People in Bible times also endured the death of their children. After all, the wages of sin is death, and since all sin, all will die. Already in Genesis 4, we learn of Adam and Eve's son Abel, who was murdered by his brother Cain. David also endured the death of children. One was the infant child he had with Bathsheba after he had Uriah the Hittite killed. When David heard of the death of his child he said, "While the child was still alive, I fasted and wept, for I said, 'Who knows whether the LORD will be gracious to me, and that the child may live?' But now he is dead. Why should I fast? Can I bring him back again? I shall go to him, but he will not return to me" (2 Samuel 12:22–23). When our daughter Catherine died, I read 2 Samuel 12:22–23 over and over. Unlike David, though, I wept each time I read it. I focused only on myself. Family and friends were wonderful to us then, comforting and loving us, helping us to get through the pain.

When I share our story with others, I discover miscarriages are fairly common. Many others share the same experience. As one large family, we mourn together and then comfort one another.

The child David had with Bathsheba wasn't David's only child who preceded him in death. Absalom also did. When David heard of the death of Absalom he says, "O my son Absalom, my son, my son Absalom! Would I had died instead of you" (2 Samuel 18:33). Whatever the specific hardship David endured in verse 1 of the psalm, we know he at least endured death of his children, possibly the worst thing any parent will ever have to endure. Yet in spite of David's hardships, he remained faithful to God. He even swore an oath to build God's temple (Psalm 132:2–5; 2 Samuel 7:27). David's plan was noble; it wasn't self-centered. He longed for a dwelling place for God.

By faith we realize that God's plans are better for us than our plans. Yet in the moment in which we live our lives, we don't understand His plans for us, and we grow tired of them. We grow tired of Him disciplining and molding us. We grow tired of the notion that God disciplines those He loves. Can't He just leave us alone for a little while and let us live our own lives? Can't He just let us be our own gods and do whatever we want?

Thanks be to God, however, He doesn't leave us alone to follow our own whimsical desires. We would surely go to hell were He not to seek us out relentlessly. Like David and me, He endured the death of His child, our Savior Jesus Christ. Unlike David and me, though, the death of His child had the added burden of our sins attached. His relentless searching cost Him His only Son.

David knew the tabernacle was temporary. Solomon's temple ultimately fell and was destroyed because it was also temporary. As we know, the permanent temple wasn't from this world—nothing in this world is permanent. It came from heaven. Christ Jesus came down from heaven and became our permanent temple, the temple of God in human flesh. Sure, this temple was destroyed on the cross, but for only three days. Christ Jesus raised Himself (John 2:19–22), never to be destroyed again. In Solomon's temple, the people were separated from God by a huge curtain. Jesus ripped that barrier just as His body was being ripped for us. In His resurrected temple, there is no barrier separating us from the love of God in Christ Jesus.

When Catherine died, I separated myself from God. Was I still a Christian? Would I have gone to heaven had I died then when I separated myself from God? Thanks be to God, He sought me out before I had to find out. I still think of little Catherine from time to time and grief still overtakes me—as it is right now as I'm writing this. But now instead of separating myself from Him, I draw closer to Him. He gives me strength to remain faithful to Him, just as He gave David strength to remain faithful. I cling to Him because He is my only hope. Paul says in Romans 5:3–5 that we can rejoice in our suffering, as it ultimately leads to hope. Hope does not disappoint, for Christ Jesus is our permanent temple, the temple of our resurrection.

....

[This temple] came from heaven. Christ Jesus came down from heaven and became our permanent temple, the temple of God in human flesh.

Prayer: Dear God, Your Son suffered for my salvation. When I endure hardship, especially the loss of a loved one, help me to turn to Your Word and Sacraments, and fill me with Jesus' resurrection power and peace. In His holy name. Amen.

....

Monday

DAILY STUDY QUESTIONS
Psalm 132:1-5

1. What is the greatest loss you have been compelled to endure?

2. While David certainly endured much loss and sorrow in his life, what seems to be the cause of his grief in the first verses of this psalm?

3. David yearned to be the one to build a temple for Yahweh. Why do you think this was so important to him?

4. How had David's desire to find a "dwelling place" turned into heartache and loss? (Check out 2 Samuel 6.)

5. Why is it that when we feel spurned by God (as both the author of the devotion and David did), we make the mistake of distancing ourselves from God? Why is this move so foolish?

Psalm 132:6–10

> Behold, we heard of it in Ephrathah; we found it in the fields of Jaar. "Let us go to His dwelling place; let us worship at His footstool!" Arise, O Lord, and go to Your resting place, You and the ark of Your might. Let Your priests be clothed with righteousness, and let Your saints shout for joy. For the sake of Your servant David, do not turn away the face of Your anointed one.

God's Footstool and Resting Place

In today's psalm, we are urged to worship God at His footstool. "Heaven is My throne, and the earth is My footstool; what is the house that you would build for Me, and what is the place of My rest?" (Isaiah 66:1). The resting place of the Godhead is Christ Jesus Himself. "For in Him the whole fullness of deity dwells bodily" (Colossians 2:9). When we see Jesus, we see God. "Whoever has seen Me has seen the Father" (John 14:9).

When I was younger, I did not like going to Sunday School or church. At my home congregation, Pastor had confirmation on Saturday mornings. Even though I was not old enough to be in confirmation class at the time, I was in the pre-confirmation class, called "Saturday School." So, I not only had to go to Sunday School, but also Saturday School. I wanted to be at home watching Saturday morning cartoons. There were not many other parents who forced their children to attend *both* Saturday School *and* Sunday School. Let alone, on Sunday mornings, there were not many parents who forced their children to attend *both* Sunday School *and* church. Yet mine did. I attended all three. (Should I mention Vacation Bible School in the summer . . .) My parents took me to hear and learn God's Word, to hear and learn of my salvation in Christ. "Train up a child in the way he should go; even when he is old he will not depart from it" (Proverbs 22:6).

I cannot recite Bible verses verbatim chapter and verse very often or very easily without the aid of a concordance, but I know of God's loving-kindness in my life—that He sent His Son, and that His Son willingly hung on the cross for me and all people. When I encounter non-Christians, I think about being able to tell of the Christian faith and of Christ Himself in season and out of season. That entails being prepared to give an answer for the reason of our hope (2 Timothy 4:2; 1 Peter 3:15). Creedal statements immediately come to mind—creedal statements I heard in church Sunday after Sunday from infancy on, a testament of doing the same liturgy week in and week out. Repetition in worship helps children learn and retain solid doctrine and teaching. I immediately think of the Nicene and Athanasian Creeds: "God of God, Light of Light, very God of very God, begotten, not made, being of one substance with the Father . . . " and "whoever desires to be saved must think thus about the Trinity." Such doctrines, especially Christology and the Holy Trinity, are at the heart of the Christian faith. When you encounter non-Christians, when they come to your doorstep, you will not have to think about what to say. Words will just come to you, words you have heard over and over and over.

I like to think of God's footstool as being at the base of the baptismal font, at the Communion rail, and at the base of the pulpit. All of these places are places where Christ is, where He promises to be. He does not promise to be anywhere else. Sure, we can look at nature and see the glory and splendor of God, but there is no forgiveness in glory and splendor. Forgiveness is found only in the cross of Christ. Therefore, I also like to think of God's footstool as being at the base of the cross. I imagine myself sitting before the cross watching my Savior take all my sin, my hurt, and my sadness. The cross came to me at my Baptism. The water from His pierced side flowed over me. My sins were washed away. The cross comes to me at the Communion rail. He gives a portion of His body and blood for me to eat and to drink. My sins are fed and drunk away. The cross comes to me at the pulpit. "Father, forgive them." My sins are spoken away, and I am declared righteous.

The Law always accuses (*lex semper accusat*). It never relents. It never leaves me alone. It is in my body and written on my heart. "The work of the law is written on their hearts" (Romans 2:15). There is no peace in the Law. Wherever we roam, we cannot roam away from the Law and from our sinful nature. There is no place to run except to the base of the cross. We are always being accused yet always being forgiven. We cannot escape simultaneously being saint and sinner. At the foot of the cross we can keep our eyes focused on Christ, the author and perfecter of our faith (Hebrews 12:2). Worship becomes a cycle of always repenting of our 100 percent sinner-hood and always rejoicing in the forgiveness of our 100 percent sainthood.

Now that I am older, I am thankful that my parents dragged me to Saturday School, to Sunday School, and to church. They fulfilled the obligation God gave them of raising me in the one true faith. I owe a lot to my parents, perhaps my very salvation. I might not be a Christian today, were it not for them (and the Holy Spirit). It is impossible for me to think of myself outside of the sinner/saint dichotomy. Nor can I think of worship outside of its sacramental nature. Christ is present, and He offers forgiveness freely to all who believe. Following my parents' lead, I take my children to Sunday School and church. And just like me, they often complain that they do not want to go. Yet hopefully, also like me, they will remain in the one true faith.

....

Now that I am older, I am thankful that my parents dragged me to Saturday School, to Sunday School, and to church. They fulfilled the obligation God gave them.

Prayer: Dear Lord, thank You for those who were instrumental in my life in bringing me to faith. Help me to be the man I need to be in order to bring others to Your footstool and Your resting place, Jesus Christ. In His name I pray. Amen.

....

DAILY STUDY QUESTIONS
Psalm 132:6-10

1. What were some things you did purely under parental compulsion that you now value?

2. How is the attitude of the worshipers in the verses of today's psalm like or unlike your own as you think about going to church?

3. What is the "it" mentioned in verse 6?

4. What do "footstool" and "resting place" convey about God and His relationship with His people (vv. 7–8)?

5. How does a priest get clothed in righteousness (v. 9)?

Week Five **Wednesday**

Psalm 132:11–12

> The Lord swore to David a sure oath from which He will not turn back: "One of the sons of your body I will set on your throne. If your sons keep My covenant and My testimonies that I shall teach them, their sons also forever shall sit on your throne."

The Right Spot

We have all been in situations in which we had assigned seating, either explicitly or implicitly. Tickets to sporting events or concerts tell us where to sit, whereas at the dinner table our seats are merely understood. At my childhood dinner table, mom and dad always had their spots, my sisters had their spots, and I had my spot. My spot was the spot closest to the wall. I was often envious and desired my sisters' spots, as I did not like being close to the wall. Evidently, my sisters did not like sitting by the wall either. Each time I requested a temporary switch, they disagreed in no small manner.

In the Bible we read of James, John, and their mother being envious. They desired influential spots at Jesus' right and left (Matthew 20:20–22; Mark 10:35–39). They were still thinking of Jesus' kingdom as an earthly kingdom. They thought of His throne as an earthly throne. Why would they think otherwise? David's kingdom was an earthly kingdom; God promised David's kingdom would reign forever. "Your house and your kingdom shall be made sure forever before Me. Your throne shall be established forever" (2 Samuel 7:16). It no doubt seemed natural to them that the eternal kingdom would be an earthly kingdom. What a disappointment it would have been for James, John, and their mother to try and reconcile the promise of 2 Samuel 7:16 with the reality of the Roman occupation. Indeed, even today, some are still trying to reconcile what and where the eternal kingdom is. They long for an earthly rebuilding of the temple and earthly rejuvenation of the kingdom of Israel. They miss the point that Jesus Christ Himself is the rebuilt temple. They miss the point that His kingdom, the eternal kingdom promised in 2 Samuel 7:16, is actually an eternal heavenly kingdom. Jesus' throne is a heavenly throne. Jesus' spot (now) is on that throne.

Where are our spots? Our spots are where God places us. He strategically places us in spots to do good works for our neighbors. In this way, God bestows on His people earthly gifts, things to support this body and life. The best gift God gave His people was His Son, Jesus. Throughout Jesus' life, God placed Him in many places: in Mary's womb, in the manger, in the wilderness, and on the cross. Jesus willingly took each spot for us. At any point along the way, Jesus, being true God, could have simply gone back to heaven. Also, at any point along the way, Jesus, being true man, could have fallen to temptation, especially in the wilderness or at the "opportune time," that is, His Passion. In the Garden of Gethsemane, Jesus said, "Do you think that I cannot appeal to My Father, and He will at once send Me more than twelve legions of angels?" (Matthew 26:53). Instead of calling upon His Father, He endured the cross.

What was God trying to teach me regarding my place, my spot back home at the dinner table? What was Jesus trying to convey to the sons of Zebedee? Christian vocation, perhaps? Obedience? The breaking of selfish desires? Sometimes we do our tasks willingly, but often we selfishly grumble at the tasks God sets before us. We wonder why God would have us do such things. "How will doing *these things* advance God's will?" "How will doing *these things* advance *anything*?" In my case, it normally happens that soon after my grumbling, God drops the hammer of the Law on me. I repent and then try to understand that God has laid these things out before me according to His good purpose. I imagine the Law being dropped on James and John. I also imagine they repented as they learned their places were to be apostles, and that they were to spread the Gospel. What has God placed before you? The hammer of the Law strikes me the hardest, however, when I think that I, that we, would still be lost in our sin and damned to hell had Jesus not done the job God set before Him. Jesus understood His vocation of being our Savior. He understood He had to suffer and die for us. That changes my perspective—at least for a time, until I grumble again. Jesus, however, never grumbled.

After the cross God raised Jesus from the dead and placed Him on His throne. "[God] raised Him [Christ Jesus] from the dead and seated Him at His right hand in the heavenly places" (Ephesians 1:20). The Lamb once slain had been placed on yet another place, a new place, where He lives and reigns for all eternity. Thinking of our Savior's vocation—His death, resurrection, and ascension to His throne—reminds me not to focus on myself or on my desires. The least we can do is do what seems a waste of time. That mundane waste of time may be just what our neighbor needs to be drawn closer to Christ Jesus. We realize we would be lost without Jesus. We need to remember our neighbors would also be lost without Jesus. Instead of thinking of ourselves, we should be thinking how we can best serve our neighbor. How can we bring our neighbor to Christ?

We may never know what we did for anybody. We do not need to know. We simply believe that Jesus died for us, and we respond in love toward our neighbor. At the separation of the sheep and goats we will be numbered among the sheep (Matthew 25:31–46)—not that anything we did in life merited righteousness. We are sheep simply because of God's gift of faith. Jesus' keeping of the Law has been credited to us. His blood has atoned for our sins. Anything and everything done in faith is pleasing to God, regardless of the spot we are in.

....

We may never know what we did for anybody. We do not need to know. We simply believe that Jesus died for us, and we respond in love towards our neighbor.

Prayer: Heavenly Father, help me not to grumble at the tasks You set before me. Help me faithfully to serve my neighbor in love, always remembering how Your Son served me on His cross. In Jesus' name. Amen.

....

DAILY STUDY QUESTIONS
Psalm 132:11–12

1. Where was the best seat you ever occupied at a meal?

2. Who is the "Your anointed one" in verse 10? What does the prayer mean?

3. Why was it comforting to the average citizens of Jerusalem, the ordinary people, to know that an heir of David would always sit on David's throne?

4. What comfort does God's sworn promise (v. 11) have for *you* in your life, today?

5. What has God sworn to do for you?

Psalm 132:13–16

> For the LORD has chosen Zion; He has desired it for His dwelling place: "This is My resting place forever; here I will dwell, for I have desired it. I will abundantly bless her provisions; I will satisfy her poor with bread. Her priests I will clothe with salvation, and her saints will shout for joy."

No Buyer's Remorse

No one controls us. We choose where to work, what to buy, where to live, and whom to marry. Sometimes the results of our choices please us; sometimes they do not. On several occasions, I have returned items I had purchased because of buyer's remorse. It drives my wife crazy when I return things. She calls me wishy-washy. I, on the other hand, think, *Why did I spend my money on that? Did I really need it, or did I just desire it?* Advertisers spend their waking hours thinking about new ways to alter our thoughts and make us believe "we can't live without it."

I wonder if God ever has buyer's remorse regarding us. I wonder if He ever regrets sending His Son into the world. His Son didn't just buy us with gold or silver, but with His holy, precious blood. Why would Christ shed His blood for everybody? Everybody doesn't love Him. Everybody doesn't appreciate Him. I, on the other hand, love Him. I appreciate Him. I'm a good person. I go to church. I'm sure He doesn't have buyer's remorse for me. But that guy down the street? I'm not so sure about him. I bet God has buyer's remorse for him. He's a real sinner. He wronged me. He doesn't deserve God's love in Christ.

A few years ago as I was walking down the street handing out political flyers with my son, a man told me in very unkind words that he didn't care for my candidate. To say what he did around my son was inexcusable. How easy it is in our pride to start thinking we are better than other people. Instead of thinking that we are somehow intrinsically better, we need to realize that we are just as bad as they, just as bad as someone who wronged us. The guy on the street, my son, and I are all sinners. "For all have sinned and fall short of the glory of God" (Romans 3:23). God's words penned by St. Paul remind me to change my perspective from "being wronged" to "having wronged." I have wronged my Lord and my God. On Judgment Day, I will have to give account for my sin, not for the sin of the guy down the street. "And [all] are justified freely by His [God's] grace as a gift, through the redemption that is in Christ Jesus" (Romans 3:24). Christ Jesus has already stood in judgment for me and for my brother down the street. God pronounced His Son guilty and pronounced me innocent. Were God to have buyer's remorse for my brother down the street, He would certainly also have to have buyer's remorse for me.

"The Lord has chosen Zion" (v. 13). God in Christ Jesus chose to redeem all of mankind, including me and my brother down the street, in spite of ourselves and our sin. "But in Mount Zion there shall be those who escape, and it shall be holy, and the house of Jacob shall possess their own possessions" (Obadiah 17). God in Christ Jesus chose to deliver us, make us holy, and grant us an inheritance. He has delivered us from sin, death, and the devil. He replaced our sin with His righteousness. He replaced our death with His life. He replaced our love for the devil with love for Him and for our neighbor. God has totally and completely replaced our damnation with Christ's salvation.

Thanks be to God, He does not have buyer's remorse regarding us. He chose us before the very foundation of the world! Because that is true, He doesn't make us fend for ourselves now. He continues to strengthen us with His good gifts. Our inheritance is in heaven where Christ Jesus our King sits on His throne. But lest we think His kingdom in heaven is some far off place in some far off time, Christ Jesus brings His kingdom to us. He brings Himself as a portion and guarantee of our inheritance. He comes to us in Holy Absolution and Holy Communion. He feeds His people with life-giving food: "I will abundantly bless her provisions; I will satisfy her poor with bread" (v. 15). I need all the free food, all the Holy Absolution, all the Holy Communion I can possibly get.

It is true that no one controls me but me. No one causes me to sin but me. If I let my sin go unchecked and unforgiven, that is, if I reject God's free food of forgiveness in Christ won for me at the cross and given to me through the Word and the Sacraments, no one will lead me to hell but me.

With our income tax refund last year, I bought a new computer. I returned it a few days later. Yes, it drove my wife crazy. (I'm sure it won't be the last time I drive her crazy.) We needed a different computer, but not necessarily a new one. I just wanted a new one. I eventually purchased a used computer. It is still working fine, and I expect it to do so for the next couple of years. There is only one thing I truly need in my life. There is only thing I cannot live without. There is only one thing that keeps me from going to hell: Christ Jesus. Everything else is here today and tomorrow thrown into the fire. Despite what advertisers would have us believe, worldly possessions, although nice, aren't signs that God loves us. The sign that God loves us is the sign of the cross—that Christ Jesus died there and took our punishment for our sin.

....

Thanks be to God, He does not have buyer's remorse regarding us. He chose us before the very foundation of the world!

Prayer: Dear Father, I acknowledge my sinful heart and sinful desires before You. Please forgive me. Keep me focused on You and on the life I have in Christ. As Your royal priest, help me to sing for joy. I ask this in Jesus' name. Amen.

....

Thursday

DAILY STUDY QUESTIONS
Psalm 132:13–16

1. What was a memorable purchase you made, only to find yourself quickly and profoundly regretting that choice?

2. Why do you think God chose Zion to be the place of His habitation?

3. How did God choose you to be a place where He dwells?

4. What would people see in you to lead them to conclude that God has chosen to dwell with you?

5. How does joy at being chosen by God show itself in your life?

Psalm 132:17–18

> "There I will make a horn to sprout for David; I have pre-
> pared a lamp for My anointed. His enemies I will clothe with
> shame, but on Him His crown will shine."

Jesus' Crown

My father wore and continues to wear hats year-round. Growing up, I never quite realized why. Finally, after many years, I had an "a-ha moment": God blessed my father with a bald head. He wears hats during the summer to keep his head from getting sunburned. He wears hats during the winter to keep his head warm. Male-pattern baldness passes down through maternal genes. So, instead of God blessing me with a bald head like my father, God blessed me with hair. I love my hair. (I think my love for hair is a reaction against my parents giving me "buzz cuts" when I was young.) I wear hats only occasionally. Psalm 132 ends with our Messiah wearing a "hat," that is, His crown: "But on Him His crown will shine" (v. 18).

All sorts of people wear head coverings. Construction workers wear hard hats. Motorcyclists wear helmets. Hard hats and helmets, of course, serve greater purposes than my father's hats. Hard hats and helmets save lives. They serve matters of life and death. Jesus' crown also serves matters of life and death. While the crown of thorns cost Jesus His life, His crown of thorns saves the lives of sinners. I, on account of my sin, shoved Jesus' crown upon His head. My sin caused His blood to flow from His thorn-pierced brow. And even after I continued to push down on His crown of thorns until I couldn't push any more, Jesus asked His Father to forgive me while He was dying on the cross. "Father, forgive them." You and I are the "them" whom Jesus asks His Father to forgive. If we are honest with ourselves, we would have to say that if we were in Jerusalem in roughly AD 30, we would have cried "Free Barabbas" and "Crucify Jesus." And yet, Jesus showed how much He loved us by staying on that cross until He breathed His last: "Father, into Your hands I commit My spirit" (Luke 23:46). His final breath was crucial. Genesis 2:7 tells us that God breathed life into Adam. Breath is key to life. Any offering less than the last breath of the Second Adam, Christ Jesus, would not have been acceptable to God.

Before Jesus died, Pilate's soldiers crowned Him (John 19:2) and mocked Him saying, "Hail, King of the Jews!" (John 19:3). Pilate himself presented Jesus as King: "Behold the man!" (John 19:5). Little did they know the veracity of their statements. When Jesus died, however, at least one soldier confessed, "Truly this man was the Son of God!" (Mark 15:39). Commentators note that the centurion at the cross might not have believed that Jesus actually was the Son of God or a son of the gods. It's irrelevant to us whether the centurion believed or not. (Hopefully he did, and now he is in heaven.) What is especially noteworthy is that God used the voice of the soldiers ("Hail, King of the Jews" and "Truly this man was the Son of God") to proclaim His truth—He always works through means. Jesus was and continues to be King. Jesus was and continues to be the Son of God.

When Pilate asked Jesus about His kingdom, He responded, "My kingdom is not of this world. . . . My kingdom is not from the world" (John 18:36). His kingship is not like earthly kingships. Jesus is unlike other kings. Throughout history, earthly kings have focused on self-preservation. Intrigue and assassinations within royal families were common during medieval Europe, for example. Jesus, on the other hand, focused on our eternal preservation. What earthly king has ever fought on the front lines of battle, much less sacrificed his life for his people? Normally earthly kings stayed well behind the front lines while their army fought for them. Jesus sacrificed Himself on behalf of His subjects. Earthly kings wear crowns as signs of power and prestige. Jesus wore His crown as a sign of humility. Only later, after He conquered death did He reveal His true power—He broke the tomb and ascended to His throne at the right hand of God. The crown of thorns He wore on the day of His death was a testament that He is our eternal king. The crown He now wears, whether still thorny or not, shines (Psalm 132:18). The light that came into the world (John 1) shines in all its glory. St. Paul tells us that Jesus emptied Himself and made Himself nothing (Philippians 2:7); He humbled Himself to death on the cross (v. 8). Now raised from the dead and ascended into heaven, He no longer conceals His glory.

Helmets completely cover the most vulnerable part of our body—the tops of our heads. Any blow or major trauma to our heads would surely kill us. Jesus' crown of thorns left the top of his head exposed. Jesus was most vulnerable during His trial and Passion. The devil took his best shot at Jesus on Good Friday, when Jesus was most vulnerable. The devil thought he had destroyed the Son of God. Little did the devil know that killing the Son of God was actually God's plan for our salvation. Little did the devil know that Jesus was going to rise three days later. Had Jesus not worn His crown to the cross, we would be damned for all eternity. The head coverings of my father, construction workers, and motorcyclists protect their heads on this side of eternity. Jesus' crown protects our heads and our entire body and souls from the eternal fire. Yes, it even protects my hair from being singed.

"But He was wounded for our transgressions; He was crushed for our iniquities; upon Him was the chastisement that brought us peace, and with His stripes we are healed" (Isaiah 53:5). Thanks be to God for Jesus' shining crown!

....

The devil thought he had destroyed the Son of God. Little did the devil know that killing the Son of God was actually God's plan for our salvation.

Prayer: Dear Lord Jesus, thank You for wearing Your crown all the way to the cross and for showing Yourself to be my King. Help me to bring honor to You and Your saving name in what I think, say, and do. In Your name. Amen.

....

DAILY STUDY QUESTIONS
Psalm 132:17-18

1. Horns and crowns were common symbols of power in the ancient world. What are some symbols of power in today's culture?

2. If the horn means power and the crown indicates kingly splendor, what does the lamp represent?

3. Look carefully at these final two verses. How did the psalm about the ark and God's presence in Zion suddenly turn messianic? How are the last two verses of the psalm connected to what precedes?

4. Who are the enemies of the Anointed One? What does it mean that God will clothe the enemies with shame?

5. If the Messiah is going to share His crown with His people (2 Timothy 4:8), how should you carry your head today?

Week Five

PSALM 132

The 132nd psalm is a psalm of prayer in which
Solomon, or the people of Israel, pray for the
preservation of the priesthood and the kingdom. That is, they pray for the spiritual and
wordly authorities: for God's Word and temporal peace. For where these both stand well,
things go well. The psalmist goes on to tell how
such a prayer is not only heard, but that God
has promised an oath to preserve the kingdom
and priesthood in Jerusalem and to dwell there
Himself. He will give all blessing and grace
Himself and bring their enemies down to disgrace, so long as they also keep His Commandments and be obedient to Him. Why, however,
he called the place of God's dwelling "Ephrathah" and the "fields of Jaar" is too long to
comment on here and belongs in a commentary.

—Martin Luther

GROUP BIBLE STUDY
(Questions and answers on pp. 200–202.)

1. Share with the group a memorable time of worship when you were keenly aware of the presence of our glorious and majestic God.

2. What does David mean in verse 5 by finding "a dwelling place for the mighty one of Jacob"? How are we to make sense of the Creator of the universe needing a man to build Him a dwelling place?

3. In ancient Israel, God was manifest to His people in the synagogue, more specifically between the cherubim enthroned on the ark of the covenant (see Exodus 25:21–22). Was this only an Old Testament thing, or are there still special times, places, or things used by God to make Himself known to His people? Where should we look for God today?

4. The title of the psalm is "A Song of Ascents." How does the title fit with what is described in verses 7 and 8?

5. How does the spirit of David and the other worshipers as they anticipate their encounter with God and His holiness compare with the spirit of worship present in your church today? What accounts for the similarities or differences?

6. What is the relationship between divine promise and human responsibility? That is, how can it really be a promise if fulfillment depends on us (v. 12)? Will this promise really be kept?

7. How do verses 13–14 affirm the truth that it is not us but God who does the choosing? Why is this truth hard for many people to accept?

8. What (or who) is the horn of David that springs up in verse 17? How do the symbols of horn (strength and power), lamp (clarity, insight, and leadership), and crown (authority and glory) each apply to God's Anointed One? That is, in what ways does Jesus show each one to us during His earthly ministry?

9. The bulk of the psalm revolves around God's chosen place to dwell ("His footstool" and His "resting place"). How does this theme anticipate and enhance the messianic focus of the final two verses?

10. How will what you have gained in your study of Psalm 132 enhance or change your attitudes and expectations the next time you worship?

Week Six

Psalm 144

1 Blessed be the LORD, my rock,
who trains my hands for war,
and my fingers for battle;

2 He is my steadfast love and my fortress,
my stronghold and my deliverer,
my shield and He in whom I take refuge,
who subdues peoples under me.

3 O LORD, what is man that You regard him,
or the son of man that You think of him?

4 Man is like a breath;
his days are like a passing shadow.

5 Bow Your heavens, O LORD, and come down!
Touch the mountains so that they smoke!

6 Flash forth the lightning and scatter them;
send out Your arrows and rout them!

7 Stretch out Your hand from on high;
rescue me and deliver me from the many waters,
from the hand of foreigners,

8 whose mouths speak lies
and whose right hand is a right hand of falsehood.

9 I will sing a new song to You, O God;
upon a ten-stringed harp I will play to You,

10 who gives victory to kings,
who rescues David His servant from the cruel sword.

11 Rescue me and deliver me
from the hand of foreigners,

whose mouths speak lies
and whose right hand is a right hand of falsehood.

[12] May our sons in their youth
be like plants full grown,
our daughters like corner pillars
cut for the structure of a palace;

[13] may our granaries be full,
providing all kinds of produce;
may our sheep bring forth thousands
and ten thousands in our fields;

[14] may our cattle be heavy with young,
suffering no mishap or failure in bearing;
may there be no cry of distress in our streets!

[15] Blessed are the people to whom such blessings fall!
Blessed are the people whose God is the LORD!

Matt Rovey

Psalm 144:1–2

> Blessed be the LORD, my rock, who trains my hands for war, and my fingers for battle; He is my steadfast love and my fortress, my stronghold and my deliverer, my shield and He in whom I take refuge, who subdues peoples under me.

Crystal Clear—In the Rearview

It was a chilly December morning in Parker, Arizona (I don't think it was much over 85 degrees!). That day I packed up my old truck and began my cross-country trek to Nashville, Tennessee. I fancied myself quite a musician and songwriter and was setting off, like thousands of others, to chase that neon rainbow. I didn't know a soul in Nashville, but with youthful vigor I figured that if anyone could do it, I could. So with everything I owned in the back of that Ford truck, I headed east on I-10. I can still feel the bittersweet emotions of that day as I left my family and the farm where I grew up.

That was nearly thirteen years ago, and I now make my living in Nashville as a studio engineer, producer, and songwriter. God has blessed me with an overabundance—a wife beyond even my prayers, four amazing children, a wonderful church family, friends, and more than I need of anything.

And yet, oftentimes I find myself grumbling and worrying like the Israelites in the desert: I'm not getting the credit I deserve. . . . The music business is on the rocks—will my career sustain itself? . . . What will we do if it doesn't? . . . How can I possibly get done all that I need to get done this week? . . . Where's my Frappuccino? (Just kidding on that one.) But seriously, the music business can be political and fickle, where you're only as good as your last hit and the ends always justify the means. Many days I feel the weight of pride, jealousy, and worry bearing down on me, as the devil grabs a fingerhold here, a foothold there.

Thankfully, God is my stronghold and my deliverer, reminding me every day of His faithfulness and steadfast love. He surrounds me with family and friends who remind me what matters. A couple of years ago, at a Christmas Day family reunion in Arizona, my uncle Ron asked how things were going with my work. I responded by saying, "Really well, but I'm still working my tail off to get to a point where I can feel secure about everything." He kind of smiled and said, "You know, Matthew, the only security we'll ever have on this earth is in Jesus, and the only time we'll ever really be secure is when we get to heaven." (Don't worry, Uncle Ron, you'll get credit if I write the song!) Needless to say, you could have knocked me over with a feather!

In the Sermon on the Mount, Jesus said, "Do not lay up for yourselves treasures on earth, where moth and rust destroy and where thieves break in and steal, but lay up for yourselves treasures in heaven, where neither moth nor rust destroys and where thieves do not break in and steal. For where your treasure is, there your heart will be also" (Matthew 6:19–21).

Regarding worry, He said, "Look at the birds of the air: they neither sow nor reap nor gather into barns, and yet your heavenly Father feeds them. Are you not of more value than they? . . . Seek first the kingdom of God and His righteousness, and all these things will be added to you" (vv. 26–33).

God provides all we need and much more, and yet it's easy, to fall into the sins of worry, jealousy, pride, and countless others. It's been human nature ever since the fall of Adam and Eve. And just like those Israelites, we worship that golden calf, in whatever form it takes.

Yet through it all, God remains steadfast and faithful!

In his Letter to the Romans, Paul wrote, "For the wages of sin is death, but the free gift of God is eternal life in Christ Jesus our Lord" (6:23). *Free gift of God*! Completely unearned, completely undeserved, but given nonetheless through faith in Christ Jesus. Not reneged, not waffled on—steadfast!

God gives us all certain talents and abilities, all useful and important in building His Church. He "trains my hands for war, and my fingers for battle" (Psalm 144:1). So rather than worrying about *this*, or wishing I had *that*, I should be using my time and talents not for myself, but singing of His steadfast love and *confidently* making known His faithfulness to everyone I see, for "I can do all things through Him who strengthens me" (Philippians 4:13).

I often have the pleasure of working with a world-class studio pianist named Gordon Mote, who has been blind since birth. He can't see the keys, yet the piano seems to be an extension of his mind and soul. God has "trained his hands and fingers" for music. I am always in awe of his talent and in the way he uses his talent to God's glory. I've never once heard him complain about anything. (He always greets me with, "Matt! It's good to *see* you!") He always speaks of how God has blessed him, and he is eager to share his faith in Jesus with everyone around. My prayer is that I be more like Gordon.

Looking back, I see clearly where God led me at crucial points in my life, points that brought me to where I am today. I don't know exactly His plan for me in the future, but I know there is one. He has put me in this place at this time for a reason. Sometimes it's hard to see looking forward, but it's crystal clear in the rearview. I pray that the Holy Spirit fills me with the strength, wisdom, and faith to let my words and deeds always point to what Jesus did on the cross for us. He took all our worries, all our jealousies, *all our sins*—upon Himself and washed them clean in His blood!

What an awesome God! In all things and at all times, let us all sing, "Blessed be the Lord, my rock and my fortress!"

....

I don't know exactly His plan for me in the future, but I know there is one. He has put me in this place at this time for a reason.

Prayer: Dear God, You know all things, even before they happen. Forgive me for worrying about my life, for it rests in Your hands. Help me to use my hands and fingers to serve others and bring glory to Your name. Through Jesus Christ, my Lord. Amen.

....

Monday

DAILY STUDY QUESTIONS
Psalm 144:1–2

1. Have you ever "moved to Nashville"? What is the most daring, life-changing adventure you have undertaken?

2. What has the Lord trained your hands to do? In other words, how has He equipped you to accomplish His purposes in service to those around you?

3. Why is calling Yahweh "my rock" a compelling metaphor? What does it look like, when a man recognizes that God is his rock?

4. Along with "rock," David uses several other images to convey God's strength and the security He affords. How does calling God "my steadfast love" fit with all the other battle-related images?

5. God is your rock. What difference will this reality make for how you face the challenges of the coming day?

Psalm 144:3-4

> O LORD, what is man that You regard him, or the son of man that You think of him? Man is like a breath; his days are like a passing shadow.

Use the Time You Have

My wife, Alicia, used to work as a business consultant for Andersen Consulting (now Accenture). Not long after we were married, we had the amazing opportunity to live in Frankfurt, Germany, for a year so that she could work on a project. Needless to say, we jumped at the chance, not knowing if or when we might have another like it! Once there, we tried to immerse ourselves in the culture, traveling throughout Europe and Scandinavia at every opportunity. Our landlords thought we were crazy, because we would drive eight hours in any given direction, even if just for a day or two. To top it all off (again thinking we might never again get the chance), when it came time to return to the U.S., we didn't choose a direct flight. Rather, we went the other way around the world, stopping for a couple of days in Turkey, Greece, Thailand, China, and Japan.

Although I can't seem to remember what I had for lunch yesterday, I will never forget the wonders of God's creation that we saw during that time in our lives. I remember thinking many times, *What a huge and amazing world this is!* It is so huge, in fact, that it made us feel very small sometimes. We would be on a country road somewhere in the middle of who-knows-where, in the middle of the night, with not much fuel left in the tank, and think, *Nobody really knows where we are . . . including us!* Or we'd find ourselves in a big city, in the midst of a throng of people whom we couldn't understand (and who couldn't understand us!). Those days made me realize what a great big world we live in and how minuscule I am in the whole scheme of things.

It's no wonder that David marveled at the fact that God, who created all things in the universe, regards us at all. It's hard to comprehend that He could know, or even care to know, what's on my mind today—what's troubling me or what I'm excited about. But He does. God knows and cares for each of us intimately! Matthew

10:30 says, "Even the hairs of your head are all numbered." (Apparently God made it easier on Himself with me, cutting down my hair count by about 90 percent in my mid twenties!) Speaking to Jeremiah, God said, "Before I formed you in the womb I knew you, and before you were born I consecrated you; I appointed you a prophet to the nations" (Jeremiah 1:5). Not only does He know us, but He also knew His plan for us before we were even born!

Through our Baptism, God calls us to be His children. But as children do, we often stray. When I was a kid, my dad was tough. He laid down the law, and my brother and I knew if we crossed that line there would be serious consequences. From time to time, we tested that theory to see if it still held, and sure enough, it always did! But we also knew that everything he did was for us. Since I first became a father in 2001, it has become even clearer to me that those laws were there out of love. I can't count the number of times growing up that Dad told me or showed me how to do something a certain way, but I would have to do it my own way. He would let me make my mistakes, and he didn't have to say, "I tried to tell you. . . ." I knew it. But there was no greater reward than to see how proud he was when I learned, tried again, and got it right. Now with kids of my own, it's as though I'm watching myself grow up again. I know that sometimes I have to be tough, but at the same time, if I loved them any more, my heart would burst!

So it is with God and us. Out of love, He laid down the Law. Can you imagine how great things would be if we would just live our lives in keeping with His Commandments? But we don't, and we can't, "for all have sinned and fall short of the glory of God" (Romans 3:23). For this, there are consequences, and we're not talking about a spanking or time-out, but eternal separation from God in hell. If not for His deep love for us, this would be our fate. "The sting of death is sin, and the power of sin is the law. But thanks be to God, who gives us the victory through our Lord Jesus Christ" (1 Corinthians 15:56). Jesus became "a new Adam" for us, lived a perfect life, died as a perfect man in our place, and rose again on the third day, granting us righteousness and salvation through faith in Him. In John 10:14–15, Jesus says, "I am the good shepherd. I know My own and My own know Me, just as the Father knows Me and I know the Father; and I lay down My life for the sheep." What an amazing love!

God knows every detail of our lives, and He gave us the Bible so that we might know Him also. When I was young, my dad would gather my brother and me around his big chair and read the Bible to us. Then we would talk about what we had read. My mom read us Bible stories before bed and taught Sunday School. We always said prayers of thanks around the supper table. God wants His children to know Him, and He instructs us as parents, "Train up a child in the way he should go; even when he is old he will not depart from it" (Proverbs 22:6).

In the psalm, David says that our days on earth are "like a breath . . . like a passing shadow." With the short time we have, we can show our children no greater love than to show them God's great love for us. That also goes for all those around us. We live in a great big world, and don't have a lot of time in it. Sometimes we feel small and insignificant. But God knows us and has a plan for each of us. He has blessed us with His grace, mercy, and peace, and He equips us through the Holy Spirit to spread the good news of salvation through Jesus Christ. With thankful hearts, let's use the time we have to share that news with everyone!

With the short time we have, we can show our children no greater love than to show them God's great love for us.

Prayer: Lord God, time is fleeting and indeed waits for no man. Forgive me for those times when I have wasted days and hours in idleness, and help me to use each moment of every day to bless others for the sake of Jesus, Your Son, my Lord. Amen.

DAILY STUDY QUESTIONS
Psalm 144:3-4

1. When or where have you had an experience that forced you to confront your own smallness and insignificance?

2. The psalmist accents the brevity of man's life and the relative irrelevance of an individual life when seen from the sweep of history. How can a stroll through a cemetery accomplish much the same thing?

3. What is the value of such poignant reminders of our finitude and inconsequentiality?

4. In the face of such melancholic, dreary thoughts (thoughts that are nonetheless completely accurate and factual), where does one turn to find comfort?

5. How does the perspective on life presented in today's two verses play out in real life? What does it look like when a man takes these ideas seriously?

Psalm 144:5-8

> Bow Your heavens, O Lord, and come down! Touch the mountains so that they smoke! Flash forth the lightning and scatter them; send out Your arrows and rout them! Stretch out Your hand from on high; rescue me and deliver me from the many waters, from the hand of foreigners, whose mouths speak lies and whose right hand is a right hand of falsehood.

Come, Lord Jesus

I grew up on my family's farm in the Parker Valley of Arizona. The Colorado River winds down one side of the valley, and two very large, majestic mountain ranges guard the valley on the east and west sides. The valley is full of lush cotton, wheat, and alfalfa farms, but beyond the mountains in either direction is desert—the kind of desert you see in old Westerns, with towering saguaro cacti and mining ghost towns that make you feel it wasn't so long ago when the place was bustling with activity. Some people may think of this type of desert as God-forsaken country, but I always saw it as blessed with a beauty like no other. We would often go with friends or family out to the desert, explore some bat-filled mine shafts, cook some hot dogs over a campfire, and lay our sleeping bags on the ground for a night of talking, watching the stars, and listening to the coyotes howl. With no lights for many miles in any direction, the night sky seemed to envelop us; it felt like you could reach up and touch the stars.

Sometimes in late summer there, a huge storm would break over distant mountains, and the lightning would light up the night sky as it stretched and split like a spiderweb for as far as you could see. Seconds later, we would hear and feel the awesome thunderclap. It would just take your breath away. And when the storms grew big enough to make it past the mountain ranges and into the valley, we knew we were in for a doozy! It could be pretty scary, but I remember the peaceful feeling when the storm would subside, the clouds would break, and shafts of sunshine would shine through to the ground. Aunt Robyn would say that it looked like God "coming down" from heaven. Then came the rainbow—reminding us of God's promise to never again destroy the earth with floodwaters (Genesis 9:11). It was like a celestial display of God's fearsome power as well as of His steadfast love.

The Bible tells us, and our lives bear out, that God is not a distant god. He hears our sufferings and delivers us, just as He did with the Israelites when they were in Egypt (Exodus 3:7). In Psalm 144, David prays for God's assistance in defeating his enemies and ruling his people. He asks God to "touch the mountains so that they smoke!" God had previously done exactly that. Prior to giving Moses the Ten Commandments, "Mount Sinai was wrapped in smoke because the LORD had descended on it in fire" (Exodus 19:18). We may not have armies to defeat or people to rule over, but if not for God's grace and mercy, we would find ourselves in a battle for our very soul, with no hope of winning. Our sinful nature is our own worst enemy! How often are we the "foreigners" that David speaks of, "whose mouths speak lies and whose right hand is a right hand of falsehood" (Psalm 144:8)? We've all experienced times at work or in other activities when someone promises to do something and then doesn't or tries to build up by tearing others down, gossips about a co-worker, and so on. Oftentimes, intentionally or not, we do the very same things. We need so desperately for God to "come down" and deliver us from our sin and the clutches of the devil.

Thankfully that is exactly what He did. "For God so loved the world, that He gave His only Son, that whoever believes in Him should not perish but have eternal life" (John 3:16). Jesus "came down" from heaven as a meek little baby in a manger, becoming man in our place and bearing the burden of all our sins on His shoulders. Though I did nothing to earn or deserve it, He rescued me and delivered me. While Jesus was up on the cross, "the chief priests, with the scribes and elders, mocked Him, saying, 'He saved others; He cannot save Himself. He is the King of Israel; let Him come down now from the cross, and we will believe in Him'" (Matthew 27:41–42). But, thank God, He did not come down until the job was done and Satan was defeated!

How truly comforting it is to have a God we can call on in our times of need, to rescue and deliver us from our troubles. This doesn't mean that we won't have any troubles, but that He will be there when we do. David knew this well, and in faith he knew that God was right there with him. Psalm 56:11 says, "In God I trust; I shall not be afraid. What can man do to me?" If we put our full trust in God, we really have nothing to fear.

Now that I live in Nashville, Tennessee, the scenery has changed a lot from my younger years out there in the desert. Nevertheless, I still like to go out at night and look up at the stars or watch the lightning flash in an approaching storm. Sometimes as I look up, I wonder what it will be like on that final day, when Jesus comes down again. Jesus said to Caiaphas, the high priest, "I tell you, from now on you will see the Son of Man seated at the right hand of Power and coming on the clouds of heaven" (Matthew 26:64). In John 14:3, He promises, "And if I go and prepare a place for you, I will come again and will take you to Myself, that where I am you may be also." What a wondrous day that will be! But for now, I pray, "Come, Lord Jesus, be our Guest, and let these gifts to us be blessed."

And He does come down and bless our lives with an abundance of gifts. The greatest of those gifts is that of salvation through faith in Him, so that one day we will go to that place in heaven that He has prepared for us!

....

Sometimes as I look up, I wonder what it will be like on that final day, when Jesus comes down again.

Prayer: Heavenly Father, I long to be in Your presence and to experience Your glory. Grant me now, in this life, Your grace, so that cleansed from sin, I may bear my cross with patience as I look forward to the day when Jesus gives me a crown. I ask this in His name. Amen.

....

Wednesday

DAILY STUDY QUESTIONS
Psalm 144:5-8

1. Does lightning terrify or fascinate you? Why might it be argued that both reactions are appropriate?

2. David has clear expectations about what will happen when Yahweh comes down. How does his presentation of that coming fit with your ideas about what it will be like for God to come down to earth?

3. What is the nature of the enemies that seem to be causing David trouble?

4. What is the nature of the enemies that most afflict you in your present routine of life?

5. How does God continue to stretch forth His right hand in the cause of His people?

Week Six Thursday

Psalm 144:9–11

> I will sing a new song to You, O God; upon a ten-stringed harp I will play to You, who gives victory to kings, who rescues David His servant from the cruel sword. Rescue me and deliver me from the hand of foreigners, whose mouths speak lies and whose right hand is a right hand of falsehood.

Sing a New Song

Less than two weeks after September 11, 2001, we were in the studio to finish cutting tracks for Alan Jackson's *Drive* album. I was a sound engineer for the sessions, recording the music. The way it generally works with Alan is that he and producer Keith Stegall go out to Alan's bus and decide what the next song will be. Then Alan comes into the studio and plays the song with just an acoustic guitar, while one of the session musicians writes up a quick music chart for everyone to follow. Once the song is charted and the overall plan is discussed, all the players go into the studio and start working it up, while we in the control room get the sounds and the arrangement dialed in. We had already cut a couple of songs that day when Keith and Alan came in for the next one. I could tell Alan was a little nervous about this song. He played through it, but he kind of mumbled the words. No one could really tell what it was about. It wasn't until he got on the mic out in the studio and really sang the song that we realized what a historic moment we were witnessing. The song, "Where Were You (When the World Stopped Turning)," went on to be a multiweek number one and both the Country Music Association's and Academy of Country Music's song of the year. More important, it was a song of healing for a nation under fire, angry, and confused. Over the past ten years, I've had several "chill bump" moments in the studio, but none like that. With the terrible events of 9/11 still fresh in everyone's hearts and minds, it was difficult to get through the song, but those emotions were reflected in the power of the finished production.

The interesting thing about all this is that it almost didn't happen. Alan was reluctant to record the song because he felt that people might perceive it as "cashing in" on such a tragedy, when that was the absolute furthest thing from his mind. He had simply woken up in the middle of the night a couple of nights earlier with

158

the lyric "I know Jesus and I talk to God and I remember this from when I was young. . . . Faith, hope, and love are some good things He gave us, and the greatest is love" running through his head. He later said that he felt like he didn't really write the song—he was just holding the pen. We see many instances in the Bible and in our own lives where God works through people to accomplish His goals. Sometimes He's subtle, and sometimes, like when He called to Samuel in the night, He won't let us sleep!

God gives us all spiritual gifts and talents, and He expects us to use them and grow in them, as Jesus explained in the parable of the talents (Matthew 25:14–30). Our nation had been attacked that September day by the "hand of foreigners, whose mouths speak lies and whose right hand is a right hand of falsehood" (Psalm 144:11). Those who perpetrated such evil did so in the name of a false god—a god not of love, but of hate. These were just the type of people from whom David was asking God to deliver him. Many, many people used their talents on and following that September day in the service of God and their fellow man. I believe that through the talent of this gifted singer and songwriter and through the simple words of his song, a message was being sent that said, "Hey, anybody who does something like this in the name of their god has got the wrong god. I know God—I know Jesus, and nothing about what those people did that day had anything to do with the faith, hope, and love that He gives us!" Isaiah 44:6 states, "Thus says the LORD, the King of Israel and his Redeemer, the LORD of hosts: "I am the first and I am the last; besides Me there is no god.'" And Peter, speaking of Jesus, said, "There is salvation in no one else, for there is no other name under heaven given among men by which we must be saved" (Acts 4:12). We know who God is, but sadly, not everyone does. And that is exactly why we need to use every bit of the time and gifts that God has given us to serve Him by serving our neighbors! Jesus said, "Truly, I say to you, as you did it to one of the least of these My brothers, you did it to Me" (Matthew 25:40).

And we should do this joyfully, with glad hearts. In verse 9 of this psalm, David says, "I will sing a new song to You, O God." A *new* song. God wants and deserves our very best. It's easy to fall into the mundane routines of life and feel like we just don't have the time or energy to stretch ourselves into new paths or ministries. Or maybe we worry about saying the wrong thing, being ridiculed by others, or being politically correct. Alan's song nearly never saw the light of day because of what "people might think." But in Matthew 5:11–12, Jesus says, "Blessed are you when others revile you and persecute you and utter all kinds of evil against you falsely on My account. Rejoice and be glad, for your reward is great in heaven, for so they persecuted the prophets who were before you." And Romans 10:9 states, "If you confess with your mouth that Jesus is Lord and believe in your heart that God raised Him from the dead, you will be saved." Through our faith in Christ as our Savior, and not by anything we have done ourselves, we have been saved. We should be energized and eager to share such terrific news! Just as Peter and John in the face of great pressure were "filled with the Holy Spirit and continued to speak the word of God with boldness" (Acts 4:30), we should, in thankfulness, spring our talents into action and continuously "sing a new song" unto the Lord, our wonderful God, who rescues us and gives us victory through Jesus Christ!

....

We see many instances in the Bible and in our own lives where God works through people to accomplish His goals.

Prayer: Dear Lord, You give each man specific abilities to bless others and specific inabilities to humble him in the light of Your grace. Thank You for using me to serve my neighbor in love. Forgive me all my sins, including those known only to You. In Jesus' name. Amen.

....

Thursday

DAILY STUDY QUESTIONS
Psalm 144:9–11

1. What is a new song you have heard that especially helps you to praise God?

2. Why is it that singing is so often (and so fittingly) associated with giving praise to God?

3. In the context of the psalm, what kind of *salvation* do you think the Lord is giving to kings (v. 10)?

4. When do you find *yourself* living like an alien?

5. David was regularly known as the "servant" of the Lord (v. 10); how readily, do you think, would people apply this title to you?

Psalm 144:12–15

> May our sons in their youth be like plants full grown, our daughters like corner pillars cut for the structure of a palace; may our granaries be full, providing all kinds of produce; may our sheep bring forth thousands and ten thousands in our fields; may our cattle be heavy with young, suffering no mishap or failure in bearing; may there be no cry of distress in our streets! Blessed are the people to whom such blessings fall! Blessed are the people whose God is the Lord!

Farmers and Builders

Having grown up on a farm, and being the father of two boys and two girls, these verses of Psalm 144 are right up my alley! My family grows a number of different crops, including wheat, alfalfa, and corn, but our main crop when I was a kid was cotton. The farm is irrigated right out of the Colorado River, and that, coupled with the warm climate of Arizona, means that the growing season is year-round. It also means that a farmer has greater control over the crops. Now this is the farmer in me speaking, but cotton is an intriguing plant. Basically, a cotton plant sets its fruit, which are cotton bolls, in stages as it grows. It will grow a while, put out new limbs, and then stop and set some fruit. Then it will grow some more, stop and set more fruit, and repeat the cycle. If you manage it right, you can get a cotton plant to load itself up in three stages before harvesttime. However, if you don't control it well (give it too much water and fertilizer, etc.) you might miss the bottom, middle, or top set, or even worse, it will grow wild, putting on little or no fruit at all. This, of course, does not make for a happy farmer at the end of the season.

David prays in verse 12 of this psalm that "our sons in their youth be like plants full grown." One of the greatest blessings and responsibilities that God has given me in this life is that of raising my children. Psalm 127:3 says, "Behold, children are a heritage from the Lord, the fruit of the womb a reward." It is my joy and duty as a parent to help give my kids a foundation, or "bottom set," in God's Word—by raising them in church, Sunday School, prayer, and family devotions, by setting examples for them to see and learn. As they grow, it continues into the "middle set," when there starts to be more independence. I'm not quite there yet as a parent—my oldest is seven—but I remember this period from my youth (sorry, Mom and Dad—now I understand!). Proverbs 22:6 instructs us on this: "Train up a child in the way he should go; even when he is old he will not depart from it." And finally you set the "top crop," knowing they're ready to go out on their own and be fruitful. In John 15:5, Jesus says, "I am the vine; you are the branches. Whoever abides in Me and I in him, he it is that bears much fruit." However, He goes on to say, "If anyone does not abide in Me he is thrown away like a branch and withers; and the branches are gathered, thrown into the fire, and burned" (v. 6). It is our great responsibility as parents to bring our children to the baptismal font and keep them rooted in God's Word, so that they will be "full grown" in their faith and fruitful for God as they go out on their own.

On the farm my dad has a machine shop where he repairs the tractors and builds a lot of his own machinery. He is meticulous in the way that he builds things, and he always stressed this to me when I was working in the shop. I often wanted to cut corners in order finish a job more quickly, but he taught me that if you don't get the first steps—the foundation—right, nothing about the rest will be quite right. David prayed for God to make "our daughters like corner pillars cut for the structure of a palace" (v. 12). My wife, Alicia, certainly provides the "corner pillars" of our family structure, with a strength and spirit that amazes me. She is blessed with parents who raised her in the fear and love of the Lord. She has a serving heart, and she passes that on to our children. Paul wrote to the Corinthians, "According to the grace of God given to me, like a skilled master builder I laid a foundation, and someone else is building upon it. Let each one take care how he builds upon it. For no one can lay a foundation other than that which is laid, which is Jesus Christ" (1 Corinthians 3:10–11). He goes on to say, "Do you not know that you are God's temple and that God's Spirit dwells in you?" (v. 16). If we see to it that our children have a strong foundation in Jesus Christ, they truly will be blessed!

My favorite time on the farm was the harvest, whatever crop it would be. I loved driving the cotton pickers, watching the basket fill up with each pass through the field. I loved seeing the gin yard full of cotton bales, the seed slab piled high with cottonseed, wheat, or corn. These were indications that all our work was fruitful—"our granaries [were] full" (v. 13). I no longer live on the farm, but God has "filled my granary" to overflowing. He lovingly provides everything that my family needs, and so much more. He gives us His grace (**God's Riches At Christ's Expense**), mercy (rescuing us from what we really deserve), and peace (in knowing we are redeemed by the precious blood of Jesus). Paul told the Corinthians, "You are God's field,

God's building" (1 Corinthians 3:9). Everything we have comes from Him, and Jesus says, "Apart from Me you can do nothing" (John 15:5).

May He fill us with His Holy Spirit to be farmers and builders for Him, raising our children to be "like plants full grown" and "corner pillars . . . of a palace," for "Blessed are the people whose God is the LORD!"

....

I no longer live on the farm, but God has "filled my granary" to overflowing. He lovingly provides everything that my family needs, and so much more.

Prayer: Heavenly Father, You provide for my every need. Help me to remain thankful—and faithful—so that the bounty of Your grace flows over from my life to the lives of others. I ask this for Jesus' sake. Amen.

....

Friday

DAILY STUDY QUESTIONS
Psalm 144:12-15

1. What kind of "farm" was the home in which you were raised? How were you cultivated to become a productive plant . . . or rather, person?

2. What is the meaning of the metaphors sons as plants and daughters as pillars?

3. What is the relationship between *praying* hard for great children and good crops and *working* hard to raise great children and good crops?

4. If riches and prosperity are not the measure of a full life, and if we are not to be pursuing money but God (Matthew 6:24), how can you explain David's ardent and specific prayer for material success (children, crops, and cattle) and blessing?

5. Considering your situation in life today, what blessings have you received from the Lord *your* God?

Week Six

....

PSALM 144

....

The 144th psalm is a psalm of thanks for kings
and those in authority. David, a king who has
to wage war and rule, gives thanks to God with
this psalm. He confesses that victory, good
fortune, and success—whether in conflict or in
government—are gifts of God and do not come
from human power and ability. Little does human wisdom know how to keep subjects under
authority and to rule land and people well. For
how should he be capable of these great things
when he is nothing and passes away like a
shadow?

Instead, the Lord does this. He sends for the
lightning—sending discouraged and frightened
hearts to the army and humble hearts among
the people. Where he thus touches the mountains and the multitudes, so that they are in
fear before Him, there it is good to fight and
rule, for there victory and good fortune follow—as well as this fear. Yet how can one, being only flesh and blood, bring about this fear?
Then he prays against his own people and re-
bukes their foolishness. For the people of Israel,
having the renown of being the people of God,
were nevertheless proud, stiff-necked, disobedi-
ent, rebellious, covetous, jealous, and faithless,

as indeed they showed by their opposition to Moses, David, and other kings. And though they saw that David fought and ruled with miraculous wonders, as did Moses, yet they were no better and did not inquire about God or faith in God.

"What God? What faith? As long as we have beautiful children, houses, cattle, many possessions, and enjoyable days, we are a blessed people. And, in addition, we have prophets enough, who teach us that God's people are those for whom things go well. Those for whom things go badly are not of God." However, things do go badly for all the saints—for the reason that they trust in God.

You have now rescued me, David says, from the murderous sword of Goliath. You have given me victory over other kings. Therefore, preserve me also from this ungodly, evil, false people, who listen to neither God nor man. They are peasants and brutes, yes, truly swine, who are concerned for nothing but their own belly. It is harder and more dangerous to rule over them than to continually be at war.

He calls them foreign children, for they want to be the foremost children of God, yet they are foreigners, strangers, and worse than heathen. They praise God with their mouths, while their heart is far from Him.

—Martin Luther

GROUP BIBLE STUDY
(Questions and answers on pp. 207–209.)

1. What's the closest you have come to an extreme display of creation's incredible power (as in vv. 5–6)?

2. How many different ways does God present Himself when He comes to His people? As a group, list as many different appearances as you can. What do they have in common? What is different about them? What do they teach us about the coming of the Christ?

3. David celebrates God's provision—recognizing God as the source of his skill at warfare (v. 1). How does one come to terms with a God of peace and loving-kindness who specifically equips a man to make war?

4. David trusted God to deal with his enemies (v. 2), but he also recognized that God had equipped him to do battle (v. 1). What does this teach us about the relationship between "simply trusting God" and "doing everything in your power" so that things work out in a good way?

5. Should the kind of blunt thinking found in verses 3–4 be encouraged among Christians? What might be dangerous about emphasizing these ideas, or what value might there be in stressing the ephemeral nature of every human life?

6. David singles out foreigners for causing him trouble by their deceit and falsehood (vv. 7–8, 11). How can you understand his charge apart from an accusation that he harbors an ugly prejudice against non-Israelites? How do you reconcile David's attitude toward his enemies with Jesus' command that we are to love and pray for our enemies?

7. While the foreigners are using their mouths to spew deceit, sandwiched between is David using his voice to sing a new song to God. How can using your voice to praise God keep you from doing the alien work of speaking deceit and doing falsehood?

8. Outside the Church today, would people consider being a servant to be a position of honor? Would they consider servanthood a worthy life goal? Why is it that David (along with Paul) wears the title "servant" (v. 10) as a badge of honor?

9. Why is it that agricultural metaphors are often applied to the work of child rearing (v. 12), and what are the areas where the images overlap?

10. David clearly correlates material prosperity with God's blessing. How do we keep from succumbing to the ideas and priorities of a prosperity gospel that insists on the virtue of expecting and receiving earthly wealth and success as a mark of God's favor? How do we reconcile verses 12–15 with Habakkuk 3:17–19?

Small-Group Leader Guide

This guide will help guide you in discovering the truths of God's Word. It is not, however, exhaustive, nor is it designed to be read aloud during your session.

1. Before you begin, spend some time in prayer, asking God to strengthen your faith through a study of His Word. The Scriptures were written so that we might believe in Jesus Christ and have life in His name (John 20:31). Also, pray for participants by name.

2. Before your meeting, review the session material, read the Bible passages, and answer the questions in the spaces provided. Your familiarity with the session will give you confidence as you lead the group.

3. As a courtesy to participants, begin and end each session on time.

4. Have a Bible dictionary or similar resource handy to look up difficult or unfamiliar names, words, and places. Ask participants to help you in this task. Be sure that each participant has a Bible and a study guide.

5. Ask for volunteers to read introductory paragraphs and Bible passages. A simple "thank you" will encourage them to volunteer again.

6. See your role as a conversation facilitator rather than a lecturer. Don't be afraid to give participants time to answer questions. By name, thank each participant who answers; then invite other input. For example, you may say, "Thank you, Al. Would anyone else like to share?"

7. Now and then, summarize aloud what the group has learned by studying God's Word.

8. Remember that the questions provided are discussion starters. Allow participants to ask questions that relate to the session. However, keep discussions on track with the session.

9. Everyone is a learner! If you don't know the answer to a question, simply tell participants that you need time to look at more Scripture passages or to ask your pastor.

Daily Study Questions

Monday Psalm 89:1-4

1. Most of us learn that it is often the hard times in life when God's love is most keenly experienced and treasured. David definitely had his share of highs and lows.

2. While we certainly can offer praises to God with our hearts and our assorted skills, humans have the unique capacity of being equipped to form their praises not only with actions but also with words.

3. David had personally experienced the faithfulness of God and knew his promises to be trustworthy. What God had said, God would do.

4. As always, God does it. He makes the first move, and we respond with David in confident trust.

5. David's offspring mentioned here is, of course, the Messiah, our Lord Jesus Christ. Every promise fulfilled for, in, and through Him is a promise fulfilled for us.

Tuesday Psalm 89:5-10

1. It might take some thought, but it is a worthy exercise to take a moment to realize how God has used others to shape you and your Christian walk.

2. Certainly, such may be the case, and while you may be able to guess at those who would count you among their spiritual mentors, the truth is that we all often make a wider impact than we immediately realize—a good reminder that our actions have significance well beyond what we see or experience in our own lives.

3. It is easiest for us to think of the scene being a picture of heaven with angels and other great creatures present. Like them, we are also creations from the hand of God, but unlike that holy company, our gatherings are always still burdened with the hard reality of sin.

4. David looks at the creation and sees there ample evidence for God's holiness and majesty.

5. The answer is yes! True, we pray for our enemies and seek God's mercy for them, but we also recognize that when God works with His justice on behalf of His chosen people, it will mean the end of those who have rejected His truth, and the Christian also can rejoice in the rightness of God's actions and the triumph of His justice.

Wednesday Psalm 89:11-18

1. God's activity in our lives is consistent and more pervasive than most of us usually realize. While we may not have the experience of some overt or even subtle intervention of divine care, we can all be confident of His continual provision for His people.

2. God's glory and His grace are both reflected in the world around us. With careful attention, we can see countless indicators of God's character evident in the spectacular and the routine realities of creation.

3. A king's rule is arbitrary and capricious if it does not have a foundation in what is righteous and what is just. Conformity to His own standard of Law is a hallmark of God's dealings with us, and we find comfort in knowing that God keeps His Word and fulfills His promises with utter reliability.

4. Those who walk in conformity with God's purposes and with confident trust in His grace know the joy and security of God's favor. It is as reassuring as a toddler taking his first steps under the watchful oversight of a loving parent.

5. The Holy One of Israel is none other than the true King, the Messiah, our Lord Jesus Christ. Through faith in Christ, all who believe are Israel and claim Israel's Messiah King as their own King and Lord.

Thursday Psalm 89:19-23

1. Perhaps it was during your glory days of high school athletics, or maybe it was when "your" team won it all, or maybe it was a great success in your work or family—whatever the cause, you can relate to the sheer joy of victory.

2. We all experience multiple ups and downs in life, and at any given moment of any given day, it might be one or the other. We do live caught within the tension of two different realities.

3. The connection is twofold. We share the humanity and so the brokenness of David. But, better yet, we are linked to David through David's greater son, Jesus—the fulfillment of every Davidic promise.

4. Perhaps we are reluctant to name the satanic origin of such adversaries, but anyone opposed to God's purposes for our lives is on the side of sin and hell—a true son of wickedness.

5. With David we anticipate the day when justice reigns and such enemies are removed.

Friday Psalm 89:24-29

1. It happens to all of us. But unless the song is really a favorite, we may find the earworm that keeps recycling through our brain more annoying than cheering.

2. The idea presents several interesting applications. First, we don't ordinarily choose the thing that gets stuck; it simply forces itself into our consciousness. Then, once in place, it refuses to be ignored. And finally, sometimes in spite of our own desires and comfort level, we find ourselves sharing the "song" with those around us. All of this is eminently true of Christ's Gospel, which captures our attention and compels us to share.

3. In the Old Testament, *horn* was most likely a reference to the horns of a bull and thus a reference to strength and power. It fails to carry that same message in most twenty-first-century cultures, but a little imagination will revive the image. The psalmist makes a wonderful promise: the servant's strength and power comes from his relation to God's name—God is his source.

4. Twice God promises the gift of His loving-kindness (vv. 24, 28). In verse 25, He celebrates the fact that this servant will exercise dominion even over the rivers and sea—standard symbols for the power of chaos and opposition to God's purposes. Verses 26 and 27 stress the unique relationship of this servant, who is the firstborn of God. Which of these images is most compelling will depend on each reader's unique story and situation.

5. Only Jesus is the highest of the kings of the earth. Only Jesus is the firstborn of the Father. Only Jesus' descendants—children of God by Holy Baptism—will be established forever.

GROUP BIBLE STUDY
(Questions are on pp. 40–41.)

1. What was the best or the worst deal you ever made? Tell the group about what made that deal so remarkable.

Many men pride themselves on their negotiating ability, so stories of good deals or deals gone bad should be relatively easy to coax from your group.

2. The common biblical word for a binding agreement is covenant. *What is the nature of the covenant in Psalm 89:3? What makes this covenant uniquely different from the deals that we make?*

God promises to establish David's royal line forever. Unlike deals and contracts we make, or even other covenants of ancient times, the covenant of verse 3 is all one-sided. God takes the initiative and makes the promise, and in return He demands nothing.

3. Given the fact that David's royal lineage did not last beyond a few centuries (the Kingdom of Judah did not make it past 586 BC and Israel ended even earlier!), how are we to understand the promise of this eternal covenant (vv. 3–4) made by the faithful Lord?

This is one of the clearest indications that this psalm must be read as a messianic psalm. While David's heirs did not eternally rule on a throne in Jerusalem, the true Davidic heir, the Son of David, Jesus, rules as God's chosen King for all time.

4. In verse 9, part of the praise of Yahweh includes His control over the sea and its waves, which in the Old Testament consistently represent chaos and evil. Why might the sea be considered an apt symbol for the resting place of evil?

It might be helpful to explore a little more of the relevant Scripture. Genesis 1 tells the familiar story of creation, but what is not so familiar is the fact that the formless void of the creation story is associated with water, which is brought under control by God. In the glorious kingdom of Revelation 21, the sea is gone—evil is conquered. For the ancients, the sea was mysterious, dangerous, and uncontrollable—an apt symbol for evil.

5. Walking "in the light of [God's] face" is not a phrase Christians often use (v. 15). Describe how it feels when you walk in the light of God's face. What does it look like to others?

Walking in the light of God's face means walking in the center of God's will—doing what He created you to do. People who notice this see a man delighting to conform his will to God's will—doing the Law.

6. *The basic idea of the Gospel is God Himself intervening for the sake of His creatures. How do verses 16–18 convey a strong Gospel message? Which particular phrases in these verses declare the essence of the Gospel?*

The fact that God's people are exalted by God's righteousness is the center of the Gospel—what we could not do (achieve righteousness), God does for us. It is God's righteousness that exalts us—never anything that is our own doing. The same idea is declared with the strength, horn, and shield of man all being made sure and certain only by God's activity.

7. *This psalm, like so many, exults in the privileged position of David, the second king of Israel (vv. 19–29). What made David so special to the Lord? At what point do these words no longer apply merely to David but to David's greater Son?*

The story of David's selection is told in 1 Samuel 16, and with Samuel we are reminded that God is interested not in outward appearances but in one's heart. What was or wasn't in David's heart is not clear from 1 Samuel or from Psalm 89. Why David was chosen has more to do with God's inexplicable choice than it does with David's singularity. At about verse 25, it becomes apparent that someone more than David is in mind—One who rules the seas and who is the firstborn of the Father.

8. *Verse 28 contains one of the most beautiful words in the Old Testament, a Hebrew word that is variously translated "loving-kindness," "mercy," "love," and "steadfast love." What is the source of this loving-kindness, and what does the promise of verse 28 teach us about God?*

The *chesed* promised to the anointed one finds its source in God alone. The fact that God promises to sustain this loving-kindness for His chosen one indicates that the God of Gospel mercy revealed in the work of the Messiah is clearly at work already in the Old Testament, accomplishing His purposes for His people.

9. *Studying a messianic psalm teaches us more about our God and Savior, but beyond merely supplying head knowledge, what difference does it make for our lives to know that God's messianic plan was gaining momentum already in the time of David?*

The messianic psalms, especially Psalm 89, remind us that God's plan of redemption for His fallen creation was always at work and that we, the descendants of David and of David's Seed (v. 29), are the purpose and the fruit of the plan. To be so central to the eternal purposes of God is at once humbling and exhilarating.

10. *How will your greater appreciation for God's work of preparing the way for His Messiah make a difference in your life this week?*

While the connections may not be immediately evident, it is critical to realize that our learning about God and His plan is more than trivia. Whatever we learn about God and His purposes should make a difference for how we view our lives and how we carry out our work. Knowing our God and our place in His plan brings direction and significance to our lives. Each participant should be able to offer some thoughts on the ways that he will strive to live in accord with God's eternal purposes in the days ahead.

Daily Study Questions

Monday   Psalm 93:1

1. Most of us, even those of us without a sovereign ruler at the head of our government, have clear ideas of what goes with being a king—the main thing, of course, is unlimited power and spectacular splendor.

2. Clearly no other ruler or lord is more exalted or more regal than the Lord who created all things and now continues to rule all things.

3. The truth, of course, is that in our sinfulness none of us ever welcomes God's lordship as we should. Instead, we resist and sometimes even rebel against His rightful reign over the way that we live our lives.

4. It is helpful and even necessary to do an honest assessment of the ways in which we resist God's rule over our lives. Of course, such an exercise is also too often painful and embarrassing, yet the path of growth and maturity is always punctuated with experiences of confession and divine, royal forgiveness.

5. It is comforting to know that God is in control, and it provides significance to our daily activities when we see them in the context of God's reign—all we do is part of His overarching plan for the world.

Tuesday   Psalm 93:2

1. Some artifacts are old and fragile, and other landmarks are solid but relatively young. One that meets both criteria may require some thought.

2. "From of old" is a poetic way of saying "from the beginning of the world." Indeed, God's throne was established from before the first day of creation. The Ruler came first.

3. Every attempt to define *eternity* or *everlasting* bogs down with comparisons to time. In fact, everlasting, like eternity is timelessness. One of the most remarkable and mind-boggling truths about God is that He is everlasting.

4. God is greater than any difficulty or setback that any person can ever experience. There is *nothing* you will ever face that will exceed God's capacity to handle and overcome it. This is the source of significant comfort and assurance.

5. It is always a good exercise to recall one's identity. To be named with God's name means that eternal matters are at work in mundane living. God is doing His business—his eternal business—through us.

Wednesday Psalm 93:3

1. Even landlubbers usually have some tale of terror to tell about an incident on the water—even if it was only in a swimming pool.

2. Perhaps it is the awareness of our complete inability to control water when it rises up with its seething power that leads us to associate those sounds with terror.

3. The fact that the chaotic primordial waters were brought into submission by merely a word from God reminds us that there is no battle between good and evil. It is a foregone conclusion: God is in control and will thoroughly conquer evil whenever He chooses.

4. While the fall certainly perverted the plan, it would be incorrect to think that the creation is now in a state of complete chaos. While humanity led all of creation into a state of rebellion against God, the good hand of God's reign still extends into the world and marks of beauty and wonder are still to be found.

5. Even mowing the lawn is a strike against chaos, as order and control are imposed on what can quickly devolve into rank chaos. Much of a man's everyday work can be considered from this perspective as a fight against chaos and evil.

Thursday Psalm 93:4

1. Living in a flawed world surrounded by flawed people, it is inevitable that at some point in life we all face situations that push us to or past our ability to freely forgive.

2. It is always helpful to remember that other real human beings have faced extraordinary challenges and received extraordinary grace. This guides us more readily to forgive by compelling us to remember our own humanity and frailty that make the business of forgiveness such a necessity.

3. There is no greater mark of divinity than the delivery of Absolution. Check out Matthew 9:1–8.

4. Fantastically lofty thrones and blinding splendor are probably among the images that come to mind. The point, of course, is that God is supremely in control and reigns with unruffled equanimity.

5. Actually practicing forgiveness is probably the single best way to overcome the reign of evil. Having such a weapon should make a significant impact on the attitude and actions you demonstrate in your daily routine.

Friday   Psalm 93:5

1. While the Law can be unpleasant when it curtails our plans for immediate satisfaction of a desire, it also makes life tolerable and even brings joy when, in conformity with the Law, we arrive at the desires of our hearts and those desires conform to God's will.

2. When we violate the Law and when we conform to its demands, we experience the fact that these laws of God are not subject to discussion or debate. They stand unyielding and effective in our own daily lives.

3. Since God is the supreme Ruler, clothed with majesty and sovereign even over the chaos and evil of the primordial flood, He has the right to establish and enforce His will as law. And the rule of law was one of the most immediate experiences of God's kingship that the psalmist would have experienced.

4. The text is clear. God wants the members of His household to be holy.

5. While all of God's Law is always applicable to all of us, special challenges and even unique opportunities often present situations when it is critical to intentionally and carefully apply the appropriate portions of God's holy testimonies.

GROUP BIBLE STUDY
(Questions are on pp. 64–65.)

1. *Living in a democracy, there is sometimes a debate about who is actually in charge. Share with the group your opinion about who really has the power in this country.*

This should spark some lively thought and discussion—indeed it could mushroom into quite a conversation. Do your best to keep it in check.

2. *Why do you think that even people without a sovereign ruler as a figurehead are still interested in the idea of royalty? What is it about royalty that is so fascinating and perhaps even attractive to most people?*

Maybe it is the idea of absolute authority and power that provides the allure of royalty for those who are not kings or princes. It is worth considering the factors that make kings what they are and what it is about kings that makes us respond with respect even if they are not our masters.

3. *The first verse seems to make an abrupt change from praising God's majesty to celebrating the foundation and certainty of the created realm. Is there a way that the two thoughts might actually be related?*

Perhaps one could make the case that the majesty of God, His royal garments, is actually the created realm—the firmly established world. So when we marvel at the wonder of the world around us, we are marveling at God's majesty and acknowledging His sovereign position and royal rule.

4. *What evidence do you see that would challenge the claim that the world is firmly established? On the other hand, what evidence might you offer in support of the claim?*

While it sometimes seems like the world is coming apart at the seams and is precariously fragile, we see in nature and in the course of human affairs the sustaining hand of God still in action. Things never get quite as bad as predicted, and God always holds His creation together and directs it according to His plan; history and creation provide ample evidence.

5. *What is the relationship between God's throne being established from of old and His very essence being everlasting? Which came first?*

This is a little bit like a chicken-and-egg question. "Which came first?" is not an appropriate question when it comes to God. God simply *is*, and it is truth that His position as Ruler is identical with His being. One could rightly argue that God was

God even before the first day of creation; before time or any other part of creation existed, He was still the omnipotent Ruler.

6. *Some contend that thinking about God's character and attributes is little more than an academic exercise void of any relevance to real life. What possible real-life applications might one make from the inconceivable reality that God is everlasting?*

Having a God who is "wholly other" (that is, nothing at all like anything that we have ever encountered or can comprehend) helps us keep the stuff of life in perspective and also provides a check on the pride and "master of my own destiny" mentality that marks our lives. The group should be able to think of other ways that thinking rightly about God's nature makes a difference for the way that one thinks about and lives life.

7. *The psalmist uses the technique of personification, giving the floods a voice. What do you think the floods were doing with their voice? What does the psalmist gain by using this technique?*

Likely the floods were shouting their defiance of God's command and rule. Unwilling to conform to God's rule, evil (represented often in the Old Testament by the flood waters) shouts out its rebellion to God's command. The use of personification helps to intensify the sense of rebellion as we imagine the floods willfully defying God's sovereignty.

8. *How does an ocean whipped into a frenzy by a storm or a mighty flood sweeping away all in its path provide an apt picture of the rule and action of sin and evil in our lives? What is it about sin that feels like a flood that will not be stopped? Finally, what does this image have to do with God's majesty?*

Like a flood or an ocean that will not be tamed or controlled, so is evil when it bursts into our lives or when we unleash it by our own choices. It will not be stopped in its course . . . except by God, who alone tames the water.

9. *The devotion for Thursday connected God's mighty acts with His action of forgiving sin. How does this move substantiate the old adage that to err is human but to forgive is divine?*

Once in a while, an old saying actually resonates with divine truth (. . . okay, it's more than once in a while that the old sayings get it right). Forgiveness truly is a profoundly divine action that exceeds the ability of mere humans.

10. *What specific actions will you take in the next week to live like one who is a child of the King, conformed to the King's testimonies?*

Our sovereign God has made known His will, and it is our privilege to live according to that will—in holiness. Each participant should be able to name one or two specific actions he will try to do in the coming week to put into action the truth of the psalm.

Daily Study Questions

Monday Psalm 101:1

1. Even those who are not gifted solo singers can usually recall a time when they were part of something bigger than themselves and blended (or concealed) their voice in a chorus of praise and celebration.

2. The old adage is that singing doubles the value and power of a prayer. While this may or may not be true, it is certainly true that singing conveys more power and emotion that mere prose. A song seems to convey truth more deeply and even more accurately than mere words alone.

3. Certainly, one's understanding and assumptions about what each of these terms means and implies will shape the answer provided. Perhaps steadfast love is a chorale in a major key or a sing-along with an easy chorus, while justice is a military march or a lament in a minor key.

4. We often see the distinction as the difference between Law and Gospel. While this is one way of looking at the message of verse 1, it is also wise to recall that in the minds of ancient readers (and in the minds of careful twenty-first-century readers), God's attributes of steadfast love and justice were actually complementary. God is just, that is, He keeps His promises, and so He can be relied upon to deliver His steadfast love. The two attributes exist as complements to one another.

5. We sing to the Lord not only with our mouths but also with our lives. Consider concrete actions you can take that would resonate as praise to God.

Tuesday Psalm 101:2-4

1. Maybe you have a mouse problem, perhaps it's bats or spiders, or maybe it's some nuisance sin that keeps coming back.

2. If you think about it, you can probably easily (and uncomfortably) identify a couple of "weak points" that are too frequently the starting points for persistent sins in your life.

3. David gives several excellent words of direction. (a) Pay attention to God's way of doing things (v. 2). (b) Be consistent—what you present in public is what you must practice at home (v. 2). (c) Be careful what you allow yourself to see—don't look at what is evil (v. 3). (d) Take no delight in the actions of those who do not

follow God's way (v. 3). (e) Don't think about what is evil and perverse—watch your "dream world" (v. 4).

4. Learning about the tools of righteousness is one thing, but actually practicing them is another thing altogether—most men know this all too well. It is critical, therefore, to be intentional about choosing and practicing one or two at time so that these tools or ways of living become part of everyday life.

5. God promises to come to us with certainty and regularity in the Means of Grace. In the Absolution spoken by the pastor, in the bread and wine of the Sacrament, and in the promise of Baptism, God comes to you with His grace and His gifts.

Wednesday   Psalm 101:5

1. The problem with slander is that once it gets started there is usually little or nothing that can be done to stem the flood of suspicion and reputation assassination that results.

2. Slander thoroughly destroys community. It is, perhaps, a reality not taken seriously enough in our homes, in our churches, and in our places of work and play.

3. It is not uncommon for one who is immersed in the sin of slander to exhibit the marks of pride described in the second portion of the verse. To maintain their imagined positions of supremacy, the arrogant often resort to slander.

4. Of course, the New Testament reinforces the message (e.g., James 3:5–12; Matthew 12:33–37) that what we say matters a great deal indeed.

5. While you may not have the prerogative of dealing with slander swiftly and decisively as David directed, you can still stand against the poison of this sin by rebuking it and refusing to participate in it. Determine now what stand you will take and how you will do it.

Thursday   Psalm 101:6

1. Hopefully, you have enjoyed at least one of those rare seasons in life when you were a part of a group of unified and mutually encouraging people all working with a spirit of righteousness. It is a delightful blessing.

2. Probably a big part of what made that time so pleasurable was the commitment of each person to do things that helped not just himself but all of the others. Obviously another big factor is agreement on the goal and the best way to get there.

3. Most likely, this is not David's way of saying that he only wanted "Christians" (Old Testament believers in the Lord) to be around him. His desire is for people who are upright and striving to live the right way. While this usually corresponds to the presence of saving faith, it is actually a matter of personal, individual righteousness—an issue of responsibility. In our relationships, we are responsible for living in an upright way. Whether or not we live this way does not directly correspond to our righteousness before God.

4. David knew what other students of human nature know: the company you keep has a profound influence on your own character and outlook.

5. Our Christian walk is going to make a difference in our daily way of life—yes, sometimes this even means intentionally choosing and changing relationships in order to aid your walk and enhance your own conformity to God's purposes for your life.

Friday   Psalm 101:7-8

1. We have all seen the remarkable damage wrought by slanderous words—indeed, most of us have firsthand experience of this calamity.

2. A falsehood is *any* mishandling of the truth. More than a flat-out lie is included. Any shading or even selective withholding of the truth is included in the idea of falsehood.

3. Though we are reluctant to admit it, full truth telling is often a difficult practice to follow. We are all prone to "spin" the facts or conceal the reality in an effort to put a more respectable veneer on our words or actions.

4. Sometimes "just telling the truth" can be a wicked and slanderous thing. The objective in your speaking should be to build up those around you and to enhance the reputation of those who are not present. As we learned it from Luther, "put the best construction on everything."

5. Perhaps such a stand will require nothing more than a renewed commitment to live according to your ordinary standards. Or you may recognize some areas of your life in which you have become complacent about and even comfortable with the chronic presence of what is evil. Determine now how you will handle that situation when you encounter it.

GROUP BIBLE STUDY
(Questions are on pp. 88–89.)

1. Imagine that someone does die and makes you king. What would be the best part about being a king? What would be the worst part?

As a rule, we are pretty proficient at enumerating the benefits that would attach to possessing the power of a potentate. We are less capable, however, when it comes to remembering the unpleasant and even difficult aspects of kingly rule—such as the responsibility for others under your care and the standards of majesty that God expects his king to follow. Simply "being in charge" is not always a good thing.

2. Read the entire psalm. What sort of attitude does David convey with regard to his position as king?

It is obvious that David does not see his position as king as a door to easy-living or as his ticket to a life filled with privilege and entitlement. He recognizes the weighty responsibility that lies on his shoulders and clearly has the goal of striving to follow God's standards . . . and more than that, he insists that those around him also adhere to those standards. For David, being king meant serious work and a burden.

3. Music was a critical part of the worship life of the Old Testament people of God (v. 1). What do you think is the style of music that is most conducive to praising God? If you were to compose a song of praise to God, what style would you choose?

While many people have rather narrow assumptions about what is and what isn't the best style for praising God, the truth is that the praise of God can take place in countless art forms and in a vast array of wildly divergent styles of music. (Personally, I think I'd pick reggae.)

4. Consider carefully the action plan presented by David in verses 2–4. As a group, recount each of the righteous practices suggested by David, and then discuss: which is most important, which is most difficult, which is most overlooked or neglected?

Question 3 from Tuesday's devotion offers a list of five principles one can readily glean from David's list. It should prove quite profitable for your group to think carefully about each of David's righteous actions and their potential usefulness in the life of a Christian man in the twenty-first century.

5. A better understanding of what it means to live righteously as God's man can produce many responses. Share with the group how you react when you think seriously about what God expects of you. What dangers need to be avoided when thinking about holy practices that should characterize the Christian man's life?

These words are words of Law, of course, and since we are human and fallen, the Law is not always a pleasant word to endure. It is common for men to feel guilty and burdened by an explicit word from God. Others may also recount a sense of excitement as they begin to think seriously about the difference that is possible by practicing holy living habits. The dangers are mutually exclusive. On one hand is the danger of self-righteousness and pride for the man who sees himself successfully following David's counsel. On another hand is despair and paralysis on the part of the one who recognizes his inability and failure. On still another hand (a three-handed man!) is complacency and apathy from the man who determines that such idealistic ways of functioning have no relevance for a regular guy like himself. Each of these errors needs to be addressed and defeated.

6. Too often what we condemn in others we will excuse in ourselves. How is this particularly true of the twin sins mentioned in verse 5? How do people make excuses for what is nothing more than slander and arrogant pride? Why do we so quickly excuse these sins when they appear in our own lives?

When it comes from our own lips, it is not slander; it is "just telling the truth" or "suggesting a possible explanation." And the pride that we despise in others, we cultivate in ourselves as healthy self-esteem, self-protective thinking, or savvy attitudes of successful business. There is a multitude of ways that people attempt to justify their own sin—some so subtle and well practiced as to be almost undetectable. All of this grows from the sins of autonomy and self-reliance—the original sins of our first parents.

7. David appears to set a very high bar for those who will be his personal associates. Is this a matter of personal choice, or is this God's counsel to us? How does one follow this direction while also following the mandate to extend to everyone love and mercy and to strive to bring the Gospel love of Christ to every person?

It is possible to do both at once. David's direction is God's direction, reiterated frequently in the pages of Scripture (1 Corinthians 15:33). God wants us to keep good company, and God wants us to extend His kingdom of grace to all we meet. The solution is to remember that there is a marked difference between being a close friend or business associate and being one who extends God's grace. While you bring the Gospel to everyone, you don't need to "hang out" with the ungodly and the unrighteous. Learning how to find the right balance should be a topic for some healthy discussion.

8. *David indicates a "zero tolerance" policy when it comes to deceit and falsehood. How does God's standard for truthful speaking differ from the world's standards for our speaking to one another? What would happen if you consistently practiced (and expected others to practice) God's standard of truth in every relationship?*

Clearly, God's expectation for truth telling and God's definition of falsehood do not mesh with what passes for truthfulness in our culture. It should prove quite challenging and perhaps enlightening to explore together what it might mean in your daily routine at home and at work if each participant consistently practiced God's high standard for truthful talk.

9. *While this psalm is filled with wonderful insights for Christian living and with practical advice for the man of God, it is generally considered a messianic psalm. What makes it messianic? Why is (or isn't) it surprising to find such practical material in a messianic psalm?*

The messianic nature of the psalm is readily apparent when one recognizes that even a king of David's caliber is incapable of living up to the standard of behavior outlined in the psalm. Only the Messiah, only the Son of God incarnate, is able to live consistently according to the pattern of divine kingship as expressed in the psalm. And only the glorified Christ is able to destroy the slanderers and wicked of the land so that only the righteous (achieved only by grace) are present in the eschatological city of the Lord.

10. *Considering the standard expressed in the psalm, would you have found a place in David's court? Knowing that grace does not release us from our responsibility to live holy and upright lives, which of the practices enumerated in the psalm most needs your attention in the coming week?*

On our own merits, none of us can meet the standard of righteousness outlined in the psalm. In Christ we receive not only forgiveness for our failures and inabilities, but we also receive the Spirit of grace and power that leads us into new lives marked by new ways of living. With the Spirit's guidance and prompting, it is possible to add new practices and new virtues to our lives. Each participant should focus not on a generic idea of "being better," but should identify some particular standard that will be the keystone of the coming week's activity of striving for God's standard.

Daily Study Questions

Monday Psalm 110:1

1. While we all face challenges every day, perhaps it would be wise to recognize the spiritual implications and overtones of those struggles. In fact, the enemy is at work with his hordes, seeking to derail faith and destroy God's people.

2. Indeed it is! All those who are opposed to God's way and God's will are rightly understood as enemies of the Gospel, enemies of God, and enemies of the Christian. While we show these enemies no hostility or contempt, we readily recognize that they are living at odds with God and God's purpose and so must be brought to repentance or be subject to God's wrath. The believer will give this divine verdict his hearty approval.

3. David is the initial speaker. "The Lord" is Yahweh, God the Father; "my Lord" is the Messiah. What Yahweh says to his chosen Messiah indicates the Messiah's elevated position: He sits at God's right hand, and all the world (even every enemy) is put in subjection to Him. Yahweh speaks the highest praise to this Messiah.

4. The beautiful reality is that through faith we share in all the blessings of the Messiah. His victory is our victory. We are His people, the object of His care and the focus of His saving activity.

5. As today's devotion declares, in Christ, you are God's chosen. You have nothing to fear, and you can count on every promise being fulfilled. This is cause for confident and worry-free living.

Tuesday Psalm 110:2

1. While the pious answer is that everything is always fine, and every challenge is simply a time for growth, the truth is that tough times can be tough on faith. Where is God, and what happened to His strong scepter when the deck seems to be stacked against you? Even believers can struggle with a God who sometimes seems aloof and disinterested.

2. At the start of the verse, David has taken up the narration, speaking to the "my Lord" of verse 1, speaking to the Messiah. It is the Lord God who then speaks the directive at the end of the verse: "Do what the Messiah does, rule!"

3. It is actually the Lord who stretches forth the scepter of the Christ. God establishes and substantiates the authority of His Christ. The Messiah's authority is not self-chosen or independently gained. It is given by God the Father. The Father inaugurates the Son's reign. The authority is rooted in the holy place, the dwelling place of God: Zion.

4. It is true that at the Last Day the strength of Christ will be His rightful judgment of all men and His authority to condemn sinners. But we can also see His strength in His willing submission to the Father's will and in His persistent and unfailing delivery of grace to those who were in desperate need. God's greatest strength is His capacity to save.

5. First Lutheran brought the scepter of Christ's rule into the reality of daily life by sharing love and concern to a young man far from home. It is often the simplest of tasks and gestures that effectively reveal God's reign.

Wednesday Psalm 110:3

1. Every one of us is under authority. Only God has total autonomy and freedom. Human beings are always under the authority of someone else—the list is probably longer than you realize: employers, police officers, government officials, parents, boards of directors, and so on.

2. Submission is a good thing. Even the glorified Christ is in submission to His Father (1 Corinthians 15:27–28). While abusive and incompetent authorities can make submission tough, the biggest issue is usually our own pride and desire to be our own masters.

3. As we all know from experience, the characteristics of the leader make a world of difference to those who are under the leader's authority. That the people freely and eagerly follow and even offer themselves as free-will sacrifices indicates that the Messiah has a personality, a message, and a purpose that inspire confidence, love, and loyalty in the people. The Messiah is a remarkable leader.

4. Soldiers are willing to go to extreme lengths in the pursuit of their purposes. They are also ready to set aside their own desires and impulses to live instead according to the direction of their superior officers. Soldiers have a clear understanding of their position, their purpose, and the price of accomplishing their calling.

5. The discipline and focus of a soldier are excellent habits for us to employ in our daily striving to live our lives God's way. Rather than merely letting life happen, a soldier makes sure that he diligently pursues the things that matter—in whatever part of life they happen to occur.

Thursday Psalm 110:4

1. Whether the loss of a close friend or family member, a lost relationship, or just a receding hairline, we all face the fact that things do not last. To confess eternity is clearly a matter of faith.

2. A priest is responsible for bridging the gap between God and man. Of course, this is accomplished supremely only by Christ, who as true God takes the initiative and bridges the impassible chasm of sin by His own sacrifice. Christ is *the* bridge builder . . . He is the bridge.

3. Clearly, the Messiah's primary task and identity are bound up with His work as Priest. This is even more significant than His role as King. Perhaps this was a lesson that was slow to dawn on the disciples, steeped as they were in the idea of a political messiah that was fashionable in their time. It is good to remember that the Messiah's task is the task of salvation—the work of restoring relationships, which is the work of a priest.

4. Melchizedek is fascinating on many levels. He is a king and a priest. He is from Salem, the Hebrew word for peace and a shortened form of Jerusalem. He seems to appear out of nowhere with no beginning and no end, and he receives a tithe from Abram. Taken together it is not surprising that many Church Fathers concluded that Melchizedek (meaning "king of righteousness") was none other than *the* King of righteousness, the Son of God blessing Abram and receiving Abram's worship in the tithe.

5. To have a Savior who is sovereign Lord and also the perfect mediator between God and man—and to realize that this was God's precise plan accomplishing His purpose for the creation—gives certainty in the fulfillment of God's promises and confidence in the power of the Messiah to complete His task of salvation.

Friday Psalm 110:5–7

1. Living in a perverse world as we do, even justice is perverted, so examples of injustice abound.

2. Heaped-up corpses and shattered kings present a graphic and gruesome picture of divine justice against human sin. The drinking habits noted in verse 7 seem an odd bit of trivia, but are meant to convey that the warrior has seen His task through to completion.

3. When we are honest about our own sins, the thought of being called to account should lead each of us to pause and hope for a stay of execution. On the

other hand, knowing God's grace in Christ—the surprising work of the messianic Warrior—we can anticipate that day with God's attitude. We look forward to God's kingdom of perfect justice being fully and finally established.

4. The words come from David who is speaking to his future Seed, his Lord, the Messiah. In verse 5, David speaks of the Messiah's divine support, Yahweh at the Christ's right hand, and the "He" seems to be best applied to Yahweh, who fights with and for His Messiah. What is odd is that by verse 7, without any apparent reason to change antecedents, the "He" now is best applied to the human/divine warrior who pauses to drink and who lifts up His head in a gesture of task completed.

5. The task of evangelism should never be far from the thoughts or words of God's people. Plan now how you will endeavor to declare the promises of God to someone you know who still lives in futility and darkness.

GROUP BIBLE STUDY
(Questions are on pp. 116–17.)

1. *Tell the group about the greatest leader you have had the privilege of knowing and following. What made him such a great leader?*

It could have been a coach, a teacher, a pastor, a boss, a political leader, or even a relative who provided the inspiration. Great leaders have certain qualities that make us want to follow them. Empathy, vision, commitment, and integrity are just some of the essential characteristics of a leader who is worthy to be followed.

2. *Having enormous messianic implications and significant teaching regarding Christ, Psalm 110 is one of the most quoted psalms in the New Testament. What makes verse 1 so important? What does it teach about the Messiah?*

Verse 1 packs a powerful messianic punch. In it, David describes the Lord (Yahweh) speaking to his Lord (the Messiah). In other words, there is someone else above David besides the Lord God. There is also the chosen son who is greater than David (Acts 2:34) and higher than the angels (Hebrews 1:13). This Savior is at God's right hand (Romans 8:34) and is seated in triumph, His saving task fully complete (Hebrews 10:12–13). David, then, is confessing that the Messiah will be more than human and will reign with Yahweh over all. Only God can do these things; thus David prophesies the fully divine identity of the promised Messiah.

3. *Why do you think the idea of absolute subjection is associated with being made into a footstool?*

Feet were dirty. Walking on dusty roads with sandals made feet rather disgusting. Feet were close to all the foul material that found its way into the streets. To this day, cultures of the Near East associate the soles of one's feet and the bottoms of shoes with contempt and scorn. To be made a footstool is to be utterly humiliated and put into subjection.

4. *In what sense is it true that the prophecy is being fulfilled even now? Is Christ ruling in the midst of His enemies? What about those enemies who refuse even to acknowledge His existence, let alone His authority?*

Indeed, the reign of Christ is present reality—over all people, whether they know and acknowledge it or not. The day will come when everyone will come to terms with God's reality in Christ, and on that day, the Messiah's reign will be indisputable.

5. *Verse 3 poses some challenges for translation. See how many different attempts are represented by the translations being used by different members of your group. Regardless of the direction of the translation, what is the basic message of this verse? What does this teach us about the Messiah and His role as leader?*

Regardless of the choices made by translators, the message is obvious: the Messiah inspires remarkable dedication from His people, who willingly and freely give of themselves for the sake of their leader. Certainly, the Messiah is not an aloof general, but one who endears Himself to His "troops" and who fosters in them a dedication and love that prompts remarkable sacrifice.

6. *What is the degree of sacrifice that God expects from His people? (Check out Romans 12:1–2 and Matthew 16:24–25.) How many Christians do you think actually understand and believe this?*

God calls us to give everything, nothing less. So, Christianity is never *part* of one's life. It *is* a person's life, completely and overwhelmingly. The percentage of Christians who actually grasp this truth is certainly less than 100; the group can debate how low the number might go, but must be reminded that the real point is that they themselves are also called to this exacting standard.

7. *Hebrews 7 thoroughly explores the Christological significance of Melchizedek. Take at look at the first ten verses of Hebrews 7, and list as many connections as you can find between Melchizedek and Jesus. How does Jesus surpass the person of Melchizedek?*

Melchizedek is an outstanding example of typology. A real Old Testament character foreshadows a greater New Testament fulfillment. The parallels between the Old Testament type (Melchizedek) and the New Testament antitype, or fulfillment (Jesus), are numerable and apparent. Of course, Jesus takes the Priest-King role to its fullest possible extent by being King and Priest for all people for all time.

8. *In verses 5–7 of the psalm, a peculiar thing happens with the pronoun "He." To whom is the "He" referring in verse 5; what about in verse 7? What does this teach us about God and his work through the Messiah?*

The "He" shifts from referring to Yahweh Himself who fights at the right hand of the Messiah to referring to the Messiah who drinks from the brook at the close of the battle. This easy interchangeability between the two antecedents illustrates wonderfully the union of Yahweh and His Messiah. Indeed, God and his incarnate Son—the Son anointed as Messiah—are perfectly one and are treated with a single pronoun. In other words, it doesn't matter when the pronoun shifts from Yahweh to His Christ—both are always at work in and with the work of the other.

9. *How do you reconcile this rather gory image of divine justice and messianic activity with the New Testament picture of God delivering grace and mercy through the Messiah?*

It is not legitimate to write this off as Old Testament versus New Testament. Rather, one should realize that chilling images of holy wrath and divine justice also fill the pages of the New Testament. The only way to reconcile the two is in terms of Law and Gospel. Both pictures are true and accurate and applicable; the distinction is based always and only on the presence or absence of repentance and faith—both gifts of the Spirit.

10. *The volunteers of verse 3 have receded into the background by verse 5, and it is God and His Christ who do all of the fighting. What does this mean for you, one of those willing volunteers, as you proceed into the week ahead?*

Victory is assured. God will see to that. But personal responsibility for living in a holy way is still in full effect for the volunteer. While you rejoice in God's provision and in the knowledge that the outcome is guaranteed, you also renew your commitment to live as a warrior of God. You especially renew yourself to the task of speaking God's truth to the world and to the individuals you encounter each day.

Daily Study Questions

Monday Psalm 132:1-5

1. The loss of a child is indeed a great loss. Because we live in a broken world, it is inevitable that each of us must deal with our share of losses, a severe challenge at the time.

2. The loss of children is a burden beyond comprehension; yet, in the initial verses of this psalm, the cause of David's grief is actually the knowledge that there was no fitting place for the worship of God, more specifically, there was no place for the ark of the covenant to dwell.

3. Perhaps David was driven by his overwhelming sense of debt for all of God's enormous blessings. Or, perhaps it was simply a mark of David's character that led him to put such a high priority on building God's temple.

4. Typical of much human experience, what David had intended for good ended in disaster with the slaying of Uzzah. Even three months later when David got his courage up again for a second, obedient attempt, the joy of the day was sullied by the disrespectful reaction of Michal. David knew the hard reality of living in a sin-filled world—even if he was intent on doing the right and faithful thing.

5. In usual fashion, we try to avoid or rebuff the one who causes us pain—even if it is God. Such a tactic is profoundly stupid, as only God can heal the hurt and the sorrow that we are experiencing. It is a remarkable mystery that we flee the only one who can deliver what we most desire.

Tuesday Psalm 132:6-10

1. Growing up in the church often affords a few memories of this variety—hopefully wisdom and the Spirit's work turns the memory into one of appreciation and joy.

2. With eager joy and anticipation the worshipers attend the ark as it moves from field to city. There is a sense of enthusiasm as they gather to worship—no compulsion here.

3. The "it" is the ark of the covenant. Read 1 Samuel 7, which tells the story of how the ark came to reside in rather unusual surroundings. The psalm recounts the search of the people for the ark and the joy at its discovery.

4. While the idea of supremacy and even subjugation are implicit in the image of a conqueror putting up his feet at the end of a campaign, the ideas of being settled and reliably present are also communicated. We know where God can be found, and He will always be there in unrivaled splendor and power.

5. Righteousness comes in two varieties. The righteousness of a priest before God is received only by grace for the sake of God's promise. On the other hand, a priest can also have the righteousness of living faithfully and obediently in this life, ably serving others around him. Perhaps both are being sought in the psalm's request.

Wednesday Psalm 132:11-12

1. Perhaps it was a holiday meal at home, the usual chair you always occupied, or maybe it was a special banquet in which you were the guest of honor. Whatever the place, the truth is that where one sits says much about one's position, honor, and blessing.

2. This most likely is a reference to the then-current occupant of the royal throne in Jerusalem, which may have changed at various times when the psalm was actually used during worship. The prayer is that Yahweh would look favorably on the Davidic heir and extend His promises and blessings to the present king.

3. Unbroken Davidic rule meant, at the very least, that the nation was continuing to exist. More promising was the hope that David's sons and grandsons through the generations would also demonstrate some of David's finer qualities of leadership, virtue, and piety.

4. That David will always have an heir on his throne seems to offer little relevance for Gentiles living three millennia after the fact. It is in the recognition of the fulfillment of the promise in the anointed Christ, David's much greater Son, that we find exceeding comfort. Christ will reign forever, and every promise of our Lord will be fully honored and implemented.

5. Among other blessings and promises, God has sworn to never forsake you, to forgive you your sins, to come to you in the bread and wine of the Sacrament, to sustain your faith, to lead you safely through death to life eternal, and to resurrect you on the Last Day in time for the eschatological feast in His presence.

Thursday Psalm 132:13-16

1. Though we may be reluctant to admit it, poor consumer habits or foolish purchases typically litter the memories of us all.

2. If God does not tell us why He does something, it is always hazardous to draw our own conclusions about what was in His mind. The point here is to recognize that there is often no apparent reason for the things that God does or the choices He makes. We know no more about why He chose Zion than about why He chooses each of us individuals to be members of His kingdom family.

3. God chose each of us from before time began (Ephesians 1:4). He created you, purchased and won you (cross and empty tomb), called and justified you (Holy Baptism), and now continues to sustain you (preaching and Lord's Supper). God chose you through the action of His Means of Grace.

4. While we all sin and continue to fall short of God's plan, thus putting ourselves continually in need of His forgiving grace, it is also true that God works in and through us to accomplish His purposes. The righteous garments of God's priests will make a difference, even when they are donned by manifest sinners such as we are. If you can think of nothing that makes those garments evident in your life, then it is time to consider more seriously the implications of God's call to live as a new creation.

5. Christians know that joy is supposed to be a hallmark of their lives, but too often this becomes more of an ideal or a mere intellectual idea than a truth realized in everyday life. God does not call you to plaster a fake smile on your face regardless of what tragedy or disaster you may be facing. But, at the same time, a Christian's life should be marked by joy that can be observed in the attitude, actions, and words of one who has been chosen by God. God's presence alters every part of life.

Friday Psalm 132:17-18

1. National flags and seals are certainly on the list, as well as governmental buildings, memorials, and Air Force One. Perhaps one might also consider a raised fist or a model of an atom as power symbols.

2. Clarity of vision, illumination of what is obscure, and guidance through the darkness are all associated with the benefits of a lamp.

3. Zion is the place where the Messiah's active work begins. His strength is made manifest at Zion. The psalm celebrates that God is present with His people at the ark and on Mount Zion. From these places of presence we rejoice in God's greatest means of being present with us—the incarnation of His Son. The connection is God's way of being present for us.

4. In the end, all who reject God's gracious reign are enemies of God's Christ. Even many "nice" people will be exposed as enemies of God and his Chosen One.

The weight of the guilt of sin will yield untold shame, and the hell that follows will allow no end to the shame, disgrace, and regret.

5. While humility would indicate a head bowed in lowliness and submission, the promised glory leads us to live with joyful anticipation. Our heads are held high and our eyes are turned heavenward, eagerly and confidently awaiting the first sign of Christ's appearing (Luke 21:28).

GROUP BIBLE STUDY
(Questions are on pp. 142–43.)

1. Share with the group a memorable time of worship when you were keenly aware of the presence of our glorious and majestic God.

It might be a service that was resplendent with high liturgy, an intimate gathering when you were especially struck by the holy sovereignty of the God we worship, or even an "ordinary" Sunday when the service was particularly potent for you.

2. What does David mean in verse 5 by finding "a dwelling place for the Mighty One of Jacob"? How are we to make sense of the Creator of the universe needing a man to build Him a dwelling place?

The ark of the covenant was the means God had chosen to make Himself manifest to his people. It was God's earthly throne. With David, we recognize that God needs nothing from His creatures, much less a roof over His head (Isaiah 66:1). However, we also recognize with David that the ways that God chooses to be present with us are sacred and deserve to be treated with respect.

3. In ancient Israel, God was manifest to His people in the synagogue, more specifically between the cherubim enthroned on the ark of the covenant (see Exodus 25:21–22). Was this only an Old Testament thing, or are there still special times, places, or things used by God to make Himself known to His people? Where should we look for God today?

Indeed, God does still use material, or physical, means to come to us and give us His mercy and truth. Today, God continues to come to us in His chosen ways. Through the Word proclaimed and the Sacraments of Baptism and the Lord's Supper, God continues to come to us and give us His grace and forgiveness. God is present with us in these ways just as certainly as He was present with Moses, David, and the ancient people of Israel at the ark of the covenant. God is where He promises to be.

4. The title of the psalm is "A Song of Ascents." How does the title fit with what is described in verses 7 and 8?

This psalm was likely associated with the ark's arrival in Jerusalem, perhaps even its move into the temple itself. This psalm of ascent (and others like it) rejoiced in God's dwelling with His people and the people's privilege in being able to worship God literally up in Jerusalem on the Temple Mount. As the people (including later generations of pilgrims such as the disciples of Jesus) went up to the temple, they would raise their voices in joy at the God who arose to come to their aid.

5. How does the spirit of David and the other worshipers as they anticipate their encounter with God and His holiness compare with the spirit of worship present in your church today? What accounts for the similarities or differences?

Each participant should be challenged to think about what exactly worship should be like and why. Beyond varying opinions about music and style, it is good to explore what it is that makes worship significant and a cause for anticipation and celebration. The promised presence of God is common to those in the psalm as well as to Christians today. This reality must always be the central thing driving and defining worship.

6. What is the relationship between divine promise and human responsibility? That is, how can it really be a promise if fulfillment depends on us (v. 12)? Will this promise really be kept?

This recurring question rightly often plagues us as we sort out the reality of an omnipotent God who controls all things yet holds us accountable for our choices, actions, and way of living. The remarkable thing about our gracious God is that he routinely fulfills His promises in spite of our inability to hold up our part. While we strive to be faithful within our callings, we recognize that God is going to accomplish His purposes without our cooperation or success in following the direction He provides. Yes, God's promise will be kept. Once God speaks, it cannot be otherwise. But, can man thwart this fulfillment with his willful rejection of God's grace? Indeed, he can—that is the terrifying reality.

7. How do verses 13–14 affirm the truth that it is not us but God who does the choosing? Why is this truth hard for many people to accept?

We confess with Luther: "I cannot by my own reason or strength believe in Jesus Christ, my Lord, or come to Him." This is precisely what the psalmist declares about Zion as the place for God's dwelling: it was God's choice, His desire. God is always the one who takes the initiative. This truth shatters the notion of human freedom and destroys any thought of human ability playing a role in salvation. Pride and self-sufficiency die slow, hard deaths—we want to do our part—and this truth is often resisted.

8. What (or who) is the horn of David that springs up in verse 17? How do the symbols of horn (strength and power), lamp (clarity, insight, and leadership), and crown (authority and glory) each apply to God's Anointed One? That is, in what ways does Jesus show each one to us during his earthly ministry?

The horn is the Messiah, that is, Jesus. He is the horn of David, the strength of God's King fully incarnate. The Gospels provide a multitude of narratives in which one can readily observe the strength (e.g., raising Lazarus in John 11), wisdom (e.g., debates with the Pharisees in Mark 12), and authority (e.g., teaching in Matthew 7) of Jesus as He fulfills the promise made in the psalm.

9. *The bulk of the psalm revolves around God's chosen place to dwell ("His footstool" and His "resting place"). How does this theme anticipate and enhance the messianic focus of the final two verses?*

Since God dwells with us in the person of Jesus Christ—God in the flesh—the discussion about God's dwelling place and the splendor and rejoicing that are associated with God's presence among His people applies supremely to Immanuel, God with us. The reaction of the people to God's presence at the ark and on Mount Zion should inform our response to the miracles of the Lord's continued presence with us in Word and Sacrament. The main point is simple: God's presence with us is a big deal.

10. *How will what you have gained in your study of Psalm 132 enhance or change your attitudes and expectations the next time you worship?*

When one recalls the promises of God, and the miracle of God's promised presence in Word and Sacrament, it is possible to see every time of worship as something bordering on the spectacular. Overfamiliarity, irreverence, and complacency are treacherous thieves that must be resisted.

Daily Study Questions

Monday   Psalm 144:1-2

1. Perhaps it was pursuing your dream to a distant city, joining the military, going to college, or changing jobs that led your life in an exciting/frightening new direction.

2. Though they may not be spectacular by worldly standards, every Christian (including you) has been given gifts, skills, resources, and abilities that are to be used for the benefit of fellow creatures. Don't discount what you might consider to be an insignificant gift. What God gives is never insignificant.

3. Big rocks don't move. They are consistent. They withstand enormous pressures and attacks. They protect. When a man knows God as his rock, he lives with confidence. Neither petty fears nor real threats can dissuade him from the course given by God.

4. At first blush, it doesn't seem to fit at all, which means that we might not be operating with an adequate understanding of "steadfast love." The juxtaposition of this word with the language of warfare teaches us that loving-kindness is not soft or effeminate. Steadfast love means hard service, daring sacrifice, and valiant deeds of love. It fits perfectly with the other military images.

5. The Psalms (or any part of Scripture) are never content to deliver a bit of information just to lead the reader to a deeper truth. The goal is always an altered life. God the rock makes a difference for the way you see life and live life—He brings peace and security and makes doing daring deeds a lot easier.

Tuesday   Psalm 144:3-4

1. Maybe it was on top of a mountain, in the middle of a vast crowd, or just under the stars—the creation holds no shortage of tangible reminders of our smallness and insignificance.

2. It is more than a little disquieting to realize that a person's life is reduced to a monument that soon weathers and crumbles. Not even a century after a stone is put in place will one be left alive who has more than a passing thought about the one buried beneath. Though we fight the truth, the world drives the point home: we are small and trivial.

3. The sense of smallness and unimportance is a gracious gift as it keeps one humble and grounded in the hard facts of reality. An inflated sense of self-importance is deadly to faith and is the enemy of grace.

4. This is the great question that drives most of the world, and it must be answered in some way by every living person. Nothing in the world (no pleasure, no philosophy, no cause) can overcome the hard fact of human insignificance. The solution is in verse 3—in spite of the undeniable truths relentlessly reverberating throughout creation, we *are* valuable to the Creator, and He *does* think of us. Our value is not in ourselves, but in the One who deems us worthy of His attention. And God's interest in and attention on us is proven in Christ.

5. A man who finds his value and meaning only in God's call and God's action will have a healthy self-understanding and will live a life that is not turned in on itself. That man will seek to accomplish what is waiting to be done—simply for the sake of being faithful and serving fellow creatures for as long as possible.

Wednesday Psalm 144:5-8

1. The wonders of God's creation, from lightning to volcanoes to towering tsunamis, reflect the power and majesty of the Creator. It is altogether right, then, that creatures should be drawn to these phenomena with wonder and awe as well as repulsed by the threat and terror implicit in such revelation of holy power.

2. David's ideas had solid grounding in the history of God's interactions with His people. Our understanding of God's dealing with us is further informed by the coming of Immanuel. The image of God's coming offered in John's Revelation contains elements of both—mercy for God's people, wrath and judgment for those living apart from God's will.

3. While the requested intervention of lightning and arrows evokes military images, the description of foreigners in verse 8 as being deceitful liars seems to indicate that David's adversaries were not military but perhaps political or personal foes.

4. Every man who strives to adhere to God's way of living will, as David did, experience opposition. Sometimes the threat is obvious and the enemies easily identified. More often the threat is not readily apparent, but nonetheless real. It is also good to recall that enemies can be friends or family or even self as these forces at times work to pull us away from God's desires for our living.

5. Without doubt, God is at work in the present era on behalf of His people. Besides the direct interventions that God continues to make—sometimes in extraordinary ways—we know that week after week, indeed, day after day, God is working

through His chosen means of Word and Sacrament to strengthen, encourage, and equip His people for the ongoing battles with all who oppose His kingdom.

Thursday   Psalm 144:9–11

1. Maybe the new song is an old one that you have just heard, or maybe it is one that only you have heard—a song not yet written or recorded. Songs that praise God come in an endless variety.

2. Setting words to meter and melody seems a more sublime and more spiritual means of communicating a thought—especially a thought of praise and worship. Indeed, as David knew, worship without music is never quite complete.

3. We typically assume that *salvation* means forgiveness of sins and rescue from eternity in hell. But in this psalm (and in much of Scripture) the word is being used more basically to refer to any form of deliverance accomplished by God. This reminds us that salvation is not limited to "spiritual" realities but includes also God's physical protection and His restoration of all creation.

4. In your sinfulness, it happens. You find yourself thinking, saying, or doing things that are at odds with God's will, that dishonor Him and hurt those around you. Deceit and falsehood spring from within you—you live like an alien.

5. While our status as God's servants is not earned but conferred by grace, the degree to which we practice our identity is, clearly, something for which God holds us responsible. It is a good exercise to consider the sort of person you are in your interactions with people—servant of Yahweh or deceitful alien?

Friday   Psalm 144:12–15

1. Reflection on your upbringing may generate gratitude for godly parents and the realization of efforts on your behalf that have not been fully appreciated; on the other hand, it may prompt you to thankfulness for God's merciful intervention and aid in compensating for human shortcomings and failure.

2. A growing boy and a growing plant have connections that are relatively recognizable, but a young lady as a corner pillar in a palace is probably a bit more obscure and even somewhat unattractive. The idea of being beautifully crafted and perhaps even integrally important for the "home" may be intended connections.

3. Clearly, these are not mutually exclusive activities. Absolute reliance on God for His gracious provision of all good things should always be complemented with wholehearted effort to do all that is humanly possible to achieve success in home and business.

4. It is not wrong to enjoy the blessings that God lavishes on our labor, and it is certainly right to recognize that all of those are dependent on God for their provision. While material blessings and success are not sure marks of God's favor (nor is the lack a mark of disfavor!), they are not to be rejected as somehow unholy or unworthy of the Christian. Praying for God's blessing is not necessarily proof of selfishness (though it is possible that it could be) but should be a mark of faith and piety—seeking from God what is needed.

5. Answers will vary. Regardless the circumstances, David is right: those who have the Lord as their God are always blessed, and the eyes of faith learn to see with increasing insight the volume and depth of those blessings.

GROUP BIBLE STUDY
(Questions are on pp. 168–69.)

1. What's the closest you have come to an extreme display of creation's incredible power (as in vv. 5–6)?

Tornado, hurricane, blizzard, earthquake, lightning strike, or volcanic eruption: everyone should be able to relate some "close call" or "right in the middle of it" experience with the raw power of nature.

2. How many different ways does God present Himself when He comes to His people? As a group, list as many different appearances as you can. What do they have in common? What is different about them? What do they teach us about the coming of the Christ?

In both the Old Testament and the New Testament, there are many theophanies (appearances of God). Sometimes He comes with thunder and lightning or with fire and smoke, sometimes in a still small voice or enthroned on a heavenly throne. Once it was as an infant in a manger. Common to every theophany is the reality that God is present in a way that will accomplish His purpose. We learn that our surprising God refuses to be boxed-in by our expectations and is more wonderful and overwhelming in the infinity of His being than we can ever grasp. Christ's coming will be multifaceted: wrath and judgment coupled with compassion and tenderness—all of God's full glory revealed in Him.

3. David celebrates God's provision—recognizing God as the source of his skill at warfare (v. 1). How does one come to terms with a God of peace and loving-kindness who specifically equips a man to make war?

Some would solve the problem by assuming a discontinuity between the God of the Old Testament and the New Testament God we learn of from the nonviolent, pacifist Jesus. Not only is such a portrayal of Jesus misleading, but it is also simply wrong to suggest a conflict between the God of David (Old Testament) and the God of Jesus (New Testament). It is better to realize that the purposes of love and peace can still be in view even when war is pursued—indeed a just war demands such a goal. As long as there is evil at work resisting God's plan and threatening His creation, He will provide training for warriors.

4. David trusted God to deal with his enemies (v. 2), but he also recognized that God had equipped him to do battle (v. 1). What does this teach us about the relationship between "simply trusting God" and "doing everything in your power" so that things work out in a good way?

Actively trusting God to provide and protect does not equal a laissez-faire attitude toward life. While we rely on God for everything and know that ultimately all things depend on His providential plan and oversight, we also recognize our responsibility to live faithfully, making use of all resources to accomplish what God would have us do. Trusting in God never yields inactivity. But individual fervor cannot be allowed to diminish complete reliance on God for everything.

5. *Should the kind of blunt thinking found in verses 3–4 be encouraged among Christians? What might be dangerous about emphasizing these ideas, or what value might there be in stressing the ephemeral nature of every human life?*

Popular psychology has laid great emphasis on establishing and maintaining personal self-esteem; the musings of David can be seen as rather counterproductive to such work. However, it is vital to remember that the entrance to Christian faith is always the reality of one's desperate and complete dependence on God for everything. David's sober words certainly push this harsh reality before our eyes. Even those of us who know Christ's grace and forgiveness need regular reminders of our true nature and need.

6. *David singles out foreigners for causing him trouble by their deceit and falsehood (vv. 7–8, 11). How can you understand his charge apart from an accusation that he harbors an ugly prejudice against non-Israelites? How do you reconcile David's attitude toward his enemies with Jesus' command that we are to love and pray for our enemies?*

Israel was God's chosen nation, His own people. Gentiles (or foreigners) were, by definition, not God's people. David is not making a culture of national distinction, but a spiritual distinction. Having enemies is never pleasant, but it is a reality when spiritual forces are at work—in this case, even nice people have enemies. While we hold no animosity or hatred toward our enemies and pray for their repentance and final salvation, we also recognize, with David, that an enemy of God is an enemy of God's people, and vice versa. The day will come when God will deal justly with every enemy, and we can also earnestly pray for that day's early dawning.

7. *While the foreigners are using their mouths to spew deceit, sandwiched between is David using his voice to sing a new song to God. How can using your voice to praise God keep you from doing the alien work of speaking deceit and doing falsehood?*

Singing and speaking God's praise as a regular habit not only lifts one's spirit, but it also serves as an effective hedge against the return of the deceit and falsehood that are the default settings for human beings. One cannot easily praise God and speak lies in the same breath.

8. *Outside the Church today, would people consider being a servant to be a position of honor? Would they consider servanthood a worthy life goal? Why is it that David (along with Paul) wears the title "servant" (v. 10) as a badge of honor?*

A servant lives for the sake of another—not exactly a typical goal in our competitive, self-serving world bent on wish fulfillment. Servants are appreciated, perhaps, but hardly honored. David and Paul both recognize that it is not the service, but the Master being served that makes living as a servant the ultimate goal and honor of their lives. It is also good to remember that a man living as a servant to others is doing what God created him to do—there can be no higher or more fulfilling goal than to do what God intended.

9. *Why is it that agricultural metaphors are often applied to the work of child rearing (v. 12), what are the areas where the images overlap?*

Both activities require a great deal of patience because the reward for hard work is often delayed. Farming and child rearing are both high commitment activities, demanding 24/7 attention. In both endeavors, what one invests directly affects the outcome, and it is not possible to go back and repair what is neglected along the way. While neither farmer nor father has complete control over the harvest, in each case, failure to do one's duty will have a decided impact on the outcome.

10. *David clearly correlates material prosperity with God's blessing. How do we keep from succumbing to the ideas and priorities of a prosperity gospel that insists on the virtue of expecting and receiving earthly wealth and success as a mark of God's favor? How do we reconcile verses 12–15 with Habakkuk 3:17–19?*

Although we may eschew the extremes of televangelists and writers of pop-religion who advocate a "name it, claim it" version of Christianity, the ideas (though perhaps in a tamer form) have a way of creeping into the thinking of every Christian. Good gifts are God's good gifts, no doubt, and are rightly the object of prayer and effort. Nevertheless, faith is founded on a reality and truth that transcend the transitory and fickle nature of temporal prosperity. With the prophet Habakkuk and with Paul (Philippians 4:11–13), we learn to be content and to praise the Giver of gifts in every circumstance with even meager gifts.

A Guy's Guide
to Church Lingo

Not everyone can tell a crankshaft from a camshaft, a rooster tail from a red worm, or a divot from a driver. You have to know the lingo (or at least know a mechanic, a bait and tackle guy, or a golf pro). Lingo is important, no matter the field. So, here are some commonly used Church words and their definitions, if you are not already familiar with them. After studying them awhile, you should sound like a pro. Try this: "<u>God</u> has <u>justified</u> me through <u>faith</u> in His Son, <u>Jesus</u> <u>Christ</u>." That wasn't so hard, was it?

–The Editor

Absolve—*to set free from sin.* God absolves us in the Gospel and the Sacraments. Absolution is not merely a symbol. On Christ's behalf, the pastor absolves us after we confess our sins either publicly or privately.

Baptism—*a holy act using water and the Word.* Baptism is not merely a symbol. God truly forgives sins, gives His Holy Spirit, and creates new spiritual life in this Sacrament.

Bible—*God's Word.* There are sixty-six books in the Bible. Because the Holy Spirit inspired each of the Bible's authors to write down every word in the Bible, the Bible is without error.

Christ—*Anointed One* (Greek; in Hebrew: *Messiah*). Christ is a title, not Jesus' last name. Jesus is the fulfillment of God's promise to send His Spirit-anointed Son to save us from our sins.

Church—*community of the baptized.* Can also refer to a local congregation or the building in which Christian worship services are held.

Creation—*everything that God our Creator has made.* This includes all planets and stars and satellites, earth, animals, plants, human beings, and spiritual beings we cannot see, such as angels.

Cross—*instrument of torture and death.* By shedding His blood on the cross, Jesus paid the full penalty for our sins, which guarantees that we have God's free and full forgiveness.

Eternal life—*living forever in body and soul in a right relationship with God.* Baptized into Christ, we have God's promise of eternal life, even now in this life.

Faith—*God-given trust in His promises.* Through the Gospel and the Sacraments, God gives us the free gift of faith, which trusts in Jesus alone for salvation.

Forgiveness—*God's act of setting free from the guilt and penalty of sin.* Forgiveness is applied in the Gospel and the Sacraments. Forgiveness is received by all who believe that Jesus is their Savior.

God—*the unseen, almighty, eternal Creator of all that exists.* There is only one God: Father, Son, and Holy Spirit.

Good works—*good deeds.* Ultimately, God performs good works through believers, who are motivated and enabled by His love and forgiveness in Christ. True good works will be rewarded when Jesus returns.

Gospel—*the good news of forgiveness, life, peace, and joy in Jesus.* The Gospel centers on Jesus' incarnation, life, death, resurrection, ascension, and coming again.

Holy Spirit—*Third Person of the Trinity.* Through God's Word, the Holy Spirit guides, convicts, and comforts us with truth that our sins are forgiven for the sake of Jesus.

Jesus—*Son of God and Son of Mary.* Jesus lived, died, rose again from the dead, and ascended into heaven for us. One day He will return in glory for us. Jesus is 100 percent God and 100 percent man, although without sin. See *God*.

Justification—*declared in a right relationship with God.* We are justified through faith in Jesus Christ, our God and Savior.

Law—*what God commands or forbids.* The Law restricts outward behavior (curb), confronts us with our sins (mirror), and shows us how to live God's way (guide).

Lord's Supper—*holy act using bread, wine, and the Word.* Also called Holy Communion; the Eucharist. The Lord's Supper is not merely a symbol. Jesus gives us His true body and His true blood under the forms of bread and wine to eat and to drink.

Pastor—literally *"shepherd."* God calls certain men to preach the Gospel and administer the Sacraments in His Church, most usually in a congregation.

Prayer—*communicating with God.* Prayer can be offered alone or with others, out loud privately, using written prayers, or simply from one's heart. God-pleasing prayers are sincere and are based on God's promises in His Word.

Psalms—*a collection of 150 hymns and poems in the Bible.* Written by David, Solomon, and other writers, many psalms were used in the public worship of Israel. Jesus frequently quoted from the Psalms.

Resurrection—*to rise bodily from the dead.* After dying on the cross, Jesus rose from the dead on Easter. When Jesus returns to earth, everyone who has ever lived will be raised from the dead. Those who have trusted in Him will be raised in perfect bodies that will never get sick, grow old, or die.

Sacrament—*holy act instituted by Jesus.* A sacrament is a sacred act instituted by God in which God Himself has joined His Word of promise to a visible element, and by which He offers, gives, and seals the forgiveness of sins earned by Christ. By this definition there are two Sacraments: Holy Baptism and the Lord's Supper. Sometimes Holy Absolution is counted as a third sacrament, even though it has no divinely instituted visible element.

Salvation—*deliverance.* To be saved means to be delivered from sin, Satan, and death. Jesus is our Savior; He freely gives us His salvation through the Gospel and the Sacraments.

Sanctification—*to be made holy.* After God declares us holy (justification), He makes us holy (sanctification) through the Gospel and the Sacraments.

Sin—*disobedience of God's Law.* Since Adam and Eve, all humans are born under God's condemnation for the sin that dwells within them, which leads them to commit actual sins. The only way to remove the guilt and penalty of sin is through God's forgiveness.

Son of God—*Second Person of the Trinity.* Jesus is both the Son of God and true man, in one person.

Trinity—"tri-unity," *Three in One.* The Father, the Son, and the Holy Spirit are one God. See *God.*

Word—*God's revelation of Himself.* The Bible is God's Word; so too is the oral proclamation of God's Law and Gospel. Jesus, as the Son of God, is God's Word in human flesh.

Worship—*receiving and responding to God's gifts.* God gives us His Word and Sacraments, and we respond to Him with prayers, praise, thanksgiving, offerings, and lives of service.